ongest established
nown travel brands,
Thomas Cook are the experts in travel.

For more than 135 years our
guidebooks have unlocked the secrets
of destinations around the world,
sharing with travellers a wealth of
experience and a passion for travel.

Rely on Thomas Cook as your
travelling companion on your next trip
and benefit from our unique heritage.

D0508089

pocket guides

ISTANBUL
Sean Sheehan

Your travelling companion since 1873

Thomas
Cook

Written by Sean Sh

Original photograph

Published by Thom

A division of Thoma

Company registratio

The Thomas Cook B

Peterborough PE3 8

Email: books@thoma

www.thomascookpublishing.com

Produced by Cambridge Publishing Management Limited

Burr Elm Court, Main Street, Caldecote CB23 7NU

www.cambridgepm.co.uk

ISBN: 978-1-84848-547-1

© 2006, 2008, 2010 Thomas Cook Publishing

This fourth edition © 2012 Thomas Cook Publishing

Text © Thomas Cook Publishing

Maps © Thomas Cook Publishing/PCGraphics (UK) Limited

Transport map © Communicarta Limited

Series Editor: Karen Beaulah

Production/DTP: Steven Collins

Printed and bound in Spain by GraphyCems

Cover photography © SVLuma/Shutterstock.com

CONTENTS

SYMBOLS KEY

The following symbols are used throughout this book:

ⓐ address ☎ telephone ⓕ fax ⓦ website address ⓔ email
🕒 opening times ❷ public transport connections ❶ important

The following symbols are used on the maps:

𝒊	information office	▪	point of interest
✈	airport	○	large town
✚	hospital	○	small town
⛨	police station	=	motorway
🚌	bus station	—	main road
🚆	railway station	—	minor road
Ⓜ	metro	—	railway
Ⓣ	tram		
❶	numbers denote featured		
	cafés & restaurants		

Hotels and restaurants are graded by approximate price as follows:
£ budget price ££ mid-range price £££ expensive

❶ *The magnificent minarets of the Blue Mosque*

 # INTRODUCING
Istanbul

Introduction

You probably have a nodding acquaintance with the clichés that circulate about Istanbul; the clash of cultures, if not civilisations, East meets West, and so on. Well, just leave them on the carousel at Atatürk International Airport, for they have only a historical truth and, like the Turkish currency 'upgrade' that discarded six zeros in one fell swoop in 2005, different values are now in play. Istanbul does straddle the Bosphorus – the narrow stretch of sea that, geographically, divides Europe from Asia – but the 13 million or more who inhabit the split megalopolis are exercised not with supposed geopolitical fault lines but with a perceived need for a modern transport system connecting the city's different quarters. For the visitor, though, the waters that break up the city – not once but twice – are part of its charm. This is Venice on a colossal scale, not so posh perhaps, but magnificently more blessed in its past glories, and spiced up with an elegant hedonism that surprises and delights.

Like any world city on the scale of Istanbul, there are neighbourhoods and districts with distinct identities, but even on a short visit you can dip into all of the most appealing. The old city, Sultanahmet, evocative of the worlds of the Roman and Ottoman empires, is the preferred destination for many travellers. Most of the historical and cultural attractions are to be found here, and at night, when Sultanahmet's skyline is lit up by ancient mosques and their minarets, a special atmosphere prevails. Across the Golden Horn, a narrow inlet of water that divides European Istanbul, there are more narrow, cobbled streets with flavours of the past, but also a more contemporary and cosmopolitan city. Here you will find bars, pavement cafés, nightclubs, design-focused restaurants, art galleries, food stalls and a swinging population of the young and young-at-heart.

Istanbul is a place to enjoy and remember, where the past and the present mingle effortlessly. Most astonishing for a city of its size and diversity, the people are easy-going and friendly and the safety factor is remarkably high.

◆ *The quaint backstreets of the old city, Sultanahmet*

When to go

Istanbul can be enjoyed at any time of the year, though there are advantages to being there between November and late March, when visitor numbers are at their lowest. The major sites and attractions are not plagued with coach parties, restaurants are less likely to be full and discounted rates are often available at hotels.

SEASONS & CLIMATE

Between November and late March, the days and nights can be chilly with temperatures ranging between 2° and 10°C (36° and 50°F) and sunshine at a premium. Mid-April to the end of May and the autumn months of September and October are ideal in terms of mild weather

and plenty of sunshine. From the end of May to August visitor numbers soar, temperatures range between 18° and 28°C (64° and 82°F) and there is a daily average of ten hours of sunshine.

Spring brings the opening of rooftop terraces for alfresco wining and dining, fresh fruits enhance breakfast buffets and dessert menus, and the city's green areas blossom with colourful flowers. The sound and light show at the Blue Mosque (see page 64) gets under way in May and lasts until September. The summer months and the long days of sunshine bring crowds to the city, the cultural calendar fills with events and an air of festivity characterises the bars and pavement cafés. The long days continue through autumn but the city is not as busy and there is still a lot happening on the cultural front.

● *The Bosphorus Bridge laser light show to commemorate Republic Day*

ANNUAL EVENTS

The website of the Istanbul Foundation for Culture and Arts, Ⓦ www.iksv.org, is a good source of information for the cultural events listed here and more. Check out Ⓦ www.mymerhaba.com for insider information on current and cultural matters. The following are some of the main regular events held in and around the city.

April

International Istanbul Film Festival The cinematic celebration kicks off in early April in a number of venues, mainly in Beyoğlu. Ⓦ www.iksv.org

Independence Day Every 23 April brings live music and a grand parade of children in folk costumes in commemoration of the establishment of the Turkish Republic in 1923. The event takes place on İstiklal Caddesi in Beyoğlu and begins in the morning.

May & June

International Istanbul Theatre Festival The main venue for this drama festival is currently the Atatürk Cultural Centre in Taksim Square (see page 30), but this may change in future years – check the website for details. Ⓦ www.iksv.org

International Istanbul Dance Festival Well-known international performers join home-grown talent in a city-wide festival that displays Turkey's increasing cultural prestige. Events take place between the end of May and beginning of June.

July

International Istanbul Jazz Festival The first week in July sees the launch of this two-week-long festival, which sends blue notes through many a club throughout the city. Ⓦ www.iksv.org

August
Rock'n Coke If you choose to make the 50-km (30-mile) hike to the fields surrounding Hezarfen Airport, you'll be rewarded by top-flight international bands and the usual festival side-shows at this three-day jamboree. Ⓦ www.rockncoke.com

September–November
International Istanbul Biennial Occurring on odd-numbered years (2013, 2015), this city-wide festival features exhibitions of paintings and other visual arts. Ⓦ www.iksv.org
Efes Pilsen Blues Festival A prestigious festival that generally takes place between October and November, in a variety of venues around the city. Ask at the tourist office for details.

PUBLIC HOLIDAYS
Secular
New Year's Day 1 Jan
Independence Day 23 Apr
Youth and Sports Day 19 May
Victory Day 30 Aug
Republic Day 29 Oct

Religious
Ramazan (Ramadan) commences 20 July 2012, 9 July 2013, 28 June 2014
Şeker Bayramı (Sugar Festival) is 19–21 Aug 2012, 8–10 Aug 2013, 28–30 July 2014
Kurban Bayramı (Feast of the Sacrifice) is 26–29 Oct 2012, 15–18 Oct 2013, 4–7 Oct 2014

Catching the sultan's eye

A Turkish warrior tribe called the Ottomans or Osmanlis, named after an early ruler, Osman I, conquered Constantinople in 1453 and as a consequence the Roman Empire ceased to exist. It was a momentous event in world history and the Ottomans went on to rule an enormous area that took in the Middle East, North Africa and a swathe of Europe. The Ottoman Empire, based in Istanbul, was ruled by Turkish emperors known as sultans, and Mehmet II, the sultan who conquered Constantinople, set about refashioning his new capital. He turned Aya Sofya (St Sophia), the great church built under a Christian emperor of Rome in the 6th century, into a mosque (see page 64) and ordered the building of a palatial residence and seat of government, Topkapı Palace (see page 66). The most exclusive part of his new palace would be strictly off-limits to most males except for the sultan and his family, hence its name, harem, from an Arabic word meaning 'inviolate', and the sultan's brothers would be permanent guests in a special area called the Cage, thus avoiding nasty intrigues over succession.

The harem, with over 400 rooms for the sultan's wives, concubines and slaves, was guarded by black eunuchs who were allowed to enter only during the day. Such was the secrecy surrounding the women of the harem that rumour was rife and stories spread about the ruler of the harem, always the mother of the ruling sultan, known as the *valide*. Her authority was unquestioned and while the *valide* enjoyed a life of luxury, the same was not true for the majority of the hundreds of female slaves under her control. Most of them were taken as captives from their homes in the Caucasus or from the west in Poland and Hungary and their only chance of a good life came if they caught the eye of the sultan. If promoted to the status of concubine, they had a relatively luxurious lifestyle and, if they bore a child, rose to dizzy new heights of indulgence and were given their own apartments; those who remained unnoticed by the sultan remained slaves and lived fairly desperate lives until they died.

⬤ *The most ornate surgery: the Circumcision Room at Topkapı Palace*

History

The origins of Istanbul's significance lie with its location astride an ancient trade route between the Mediterranean and Asia. The Greeks founded city-states on both the European and Asian sides of the Bosphorus and one of these, Byzantium, was conquered by the Romans in 64 BC. In the 4th century AD the Roman emperor Constantine relocated his capital to Byzantium and the city became known as Constantinople. When barbarian hordes stormed the gates of Rome a century later, the Greek-speaking and Christianised Constantinople survived in the East. A thousand years later it was still ruled by emperors who called themselves Roman and the city became the mainstay of what became known as the Byzantine Empire, enfolding the Mediterranean littoral from Spain to Syria. The Byzantine era is the context for some of the most monumental structures that visitors flock to see today, including Aya Sofya (see page 64), the church of St Sofia built under Emperor Justinian in the 6th century. Five centuries later, the empire was still pulling rank under not Buffy, but Basil the Bulgar-slayer, and a hundred years later, when western Europe had emerged from the dark ages, more people still lived in Constantinople than in Rome, London and Paris combined.

Empires come and go, however, and in 1453 it was the turn of the Ottomans to rule the roost and Topkapı Palace (see page 66) was built as the palatial pad for a reign of sultans with names like Süleyman the Magnificent, Selim the Sot and Brahim the Mad. Notwithstanding the nomenclature, the Ottomans were remarkably resilient and survived for over 400 years. It was not until the early 20th century that, finding itself on the losing side in World War I, the Ottoman Empire saw itself at the mercy of the victors.

It was the end of Ottoman rule but, when Greek armies invaded Anatolia in 1919, a resurgent nationalism asserted itself and the Turkish War of Independence led to the creation of a Turkish Republic in 1923. The young soldier who emerged from the War of Independence as the saviour of the nation was Mustafa Kemal Paşa and he was proclaimed Atatürk ('Father of the Turks'). As well as being the founder, Atatürk was the first president of the Republic of Turkey. He carried out many reforms, such as replacing the Arabic alphabet with a Roman one, encouraging a Western style of dress and unifying education through democratisation and secularisation. To signal Turkey's new identity, Atatürk shifted the nation's capital from Istanbul to Ankara.

Democracy came to Turkey in the wake of World War II and, despite military coups in 1960, 1971 and 1980 and the collapse of the Turkish economy in 2001, the country is now a stable constitutional state. Under the strong leadership of Prime Minister Erdoğan, and with 2010's staggering growth rate of over 11 per cent, outperforming both India and China, Turkey is poised once again to take a major role in regional politics. Its EU candidacy is fast slipping off the agenda, and in the wake of the 2011 Arab Spring, it is widely seen as the new model for a democratic Muslim secular state.

Lifestyle

As you would expect from a city with a population of 13 million, Istanbul is a bustling and cosmopolitan metropolis where most people are busy going about the business of living. Yet what emerges as a pleasant surprise is an impression of people not harassed by urban pressures or borne down by the stress of work but, instead, rather well adjusted to a chosen pace of life that allows for relaxation. Cups of tea and coffee are not gulped down in-between rushing off to that next deadline – though the cups are so inordinately small you could be forgiven for thinking they were designed for just that purpose – but sipped leisurely and made to last for extended bouts of convivial conversation. This is a city happier with itself than one might expect, considering the hustle and bustle and the mix of ethnicities, and there is a strong sense of people living together on their own terms of civility and sociability.

Aspects of this very public lifestyle are there to be encountered on the street and even the hustlers in Sultanahmet (see page 60) who try to inveigle you into their carpet shops do so with charm and courtesy, and if you appear cross at their antics they wonder why you are being so disagreeable. There is always time, it seems, to take a drink and have a chat and this is nowhere so apparent as in the pavement cafés and alfresco bars that litter the city when the winter cold has passed and the days are long and warm. The stupendous grandeur of three past civilisations and the minaret-studded cityscape is taken for granted by Istanbulites, who see it all as their glorious backdrop for romancing the city and making and sustaining friendships, as well as making a living and getting by.

Islam's religious festivals influence Istanbulites' lifestyles. During the holy month of Ramazan (Ramadan, see page 11), Muslims refrain from eating and drinking between dawn and dusk, but most restaurants and bars remain open. While non-Muslim visitors are not inconvenienced, it is only polite not to make a show of eating or drinking during the day.

△ *There are plenty of pavement bars and cafés throughout the city*

Culture

History provides a clue to the astonishing richness and diversity of the city's culture and the Archaeological Museum (see page 63) opens a window on the ancient background and broader context that the city has shared in for so many centuries. The millennium-long Byzantine Empire, when Istanbul was called Constantinople, a world capital and the richest city in Christendom, nurtured a flowering of the arts and created structures like the Aya Sofya (see page 64), the Hippodrome (see page 62), Valens Aqueduct (see page 78) and the Basilica Cistern (see page 63). It is the richness of this cultural legacy that makes Sultanahmet such an attractive base for accommodation in the city because this area was the heart of Constantinople and there are reminders of the Byzantine past everywhere you look and walk.

A new cultural chapter began even before the final conquest of Constantinople in 1453 by the Ottomans when Rumeli Hisarı (see page 121) was built on the Bosphorus. In the city itself, Ottoman architecture expressed itself in the mighty Topkapı Palace (see page 66) and, as part of an empire founded on the Muslim faith, in the building of the many great mosques that continue to adorn the city. Chief among these cultural highlights are the Blue Mosque (see page 64) and the magnificent Süleymaniye Camii complex (see page 78). For many, however, Islamic art is at its finest not on the monumental scale but in the intricate detail of mosaics and calligraphy, and the best place to appreciate these art forms is in the Museum of Turkish and Islamic Arts (see page 66) and the Museum of Calligraphy (see page 81). Ottoman culture also absorbed European influences and these can be appreciated in the 19th-century décor of Dolmabahçe Palace (see page 105).

⬥ *The Basilica – Istanbul's impressive medieval underground water cisterns*

MOSQUE CULTURE

Non-Muslim visitors are welcome at all Istanbul mosques and, like any place of worship, proprieties should be observed. Shoes are removed before entry and bare arms and legs should be covered. Men remove hats or caps and women cover their hair with a scarf. There are five daily prayer times, each lasting 30 or 40 minutes, during which you should not wander around devotees. The main prayer session takes place on a Friday and visiting a mosque should be avoided on this day. There is no charge for visiting a mosque but, when leaving, it is courteous to make a contribution to the donation box.

Istanbul was designated European Capital of Culture in 2010 not only for its wealth of historical and archaeological buildings, sites and artefacts but in recognition of its thriving contemporary arts scene. Pride of place goes to the waterside Istanbul Modern (see page 93), a converted warehouse with large open spaces for exhibitions of paintings, sculptures and installation art. Close on its heels are two other galleries: the Pera Museum (see page 94), which is also in Beyoğlu, and the Sakıp Sabancı Museum (see page 125), which is further out on the shores of the Bosphorus at Emirgan. The fact that the museum displays both Islamic art and leading European masterpieces makes a journey there worthwhile.

● *Enter Istanbul: worlds within worlds at the Blue Mosque*

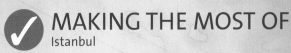

MAKING THE MOST OF
Istanbul

Shopping

Shopping is easy in Istanbul, offering variety and choices for all budgets and, while payment can be made with a credit card in most places, many shops will offer a small discount equivalent to the card company charge if you pay in cash. Bargaining is not practised in the brand-name or upmarket stores, nor is it generally expected where the price of items is clearly marked – especially with lower-priced souvenirs. However, when it comes to purchases in shops aimed at visitors, you can be fairly sure that some haggling is expected. When battling for a bargain, keep it courteous at all times and try to have some idea of what the merchandise is worth (or at least what it is worth to you). Try not to be the first to make an offer and when you do, ensure it is less than you are prepared to pay.

The Grand Bazaar (see page 76) is the most renowned shopping area for carpets, jewellery, leather jackets, handicrafts and souvenirs and you have some 4,000 shops to choose from. Bargains, though, are rare and haggling is an art form that the vendors have more skill at than most punters. The Spice Bazaar (see page 76) is smaller and can be more satisfying. For general merchandise and fashion in all its guises, pedestrianised İstiklal Caddesi is the place to start, though there are a number of interesting little shops tucked away off it in the backstreets of Galatasaray (see page 88). Here you will also find antiquities of an affordable kind as well as one-off items of clothing. For souvenirs, schlocky and tasteful, as well as handicrafts and ubiquitous carpet dealers, the streets of Sultanahmet (see page 60) await you.

In terms of what to buy, take your pick from an exhaustive range of beautiful ceramics (plates, bowls, *İznik*-style tiles), handicrafts (inlaid wood, alabaster ornaments), copperware, glassware, rich textiles (cotton, silk, cashmere, embroidered cloth, knitted goods, leather) and exquisite carpets and *kilims* (rugs). Blue glass-eye pendants, *nargiles* (bubble pipes) and miniature paintings are among the easiest and most affordable souvenirs, unless you want to take home a taste of Istanbul, in which case you simply can't beat fresh Turkish delight. Nuts in honey, *halva* (a sweet confection), spices, the national alcoholic beverage *rakı* or Turkish wine are also good choices.

USEFUL SHOPPING PHRASES

What time do the shops open/close?
Dükkanlar ne zaman açılır/kapanır?
Duekkanlar ne zaman acheler/kapanaer?

How much is this?
Kaça?
Kacha?

Can I try this on?
Bunu prova edebilir miyim?
Bunu prova edebilir miim?

My size is ...
Benim ölçüm ...
Benim oelchuem ...

I'll take this one, thank you
Bunu alacağım, teşekkür ederim
Bunu aladja'em, teshekkuer ederim

This is too large/too small/too expensive. Do you have any others?
Bu çok büyük/çok küçük/çok pahalı. Başka çeşitleriniz de var mı?
Bu chok bueyuek/chok kuechuek/chok paha'le. Bashka cheshitleriniz de var me?

Eating & drinking

Food and drink is everywhere in Istanbul and you will never have difficulty finding a restaurant or bar. The range of establishments is extensive, from low-cost *lokantas* (traditional Turkish restaurants) for quick meals to fine-dining restaurants for gourmets, and in-between there are eateries, cafés and bars to suit most moods, budgets, taste buds and food fads. Turkish cuisine is rich and varied, as well as creative enough to successfully take on the fusion challenge, and at times it blends effortlessly with wider Mediterranean tastes.

Turkish starters, mezes, constitute the most creative aspect of Turkish food because there are endless variations and few hard and fast rules about their composition. More often cold than hot, they are usually based around vegetables and fish and take the form of various purées and dips with yoghurt and salad ingredients. Served with fresh bread, a large plate of mezes can be a small meal in itself. *Börek* is another Turkish delicacy, a savoury and flaky pastry filled with anything from cheese with herbs to mince or vegetables. You may see them on a breakfast buffet, often cigar shaped. A *dolma* is any piece of food that can be filled with more food and some of the tastiest use vine leaves and peppers.

Drinking can be an equally eclectic experience and Turkish tastes take in tea (*çay*), herbal or straight, in neat little tulip-shaped glasses,

PRICE CATEGORIES

Restaurant ratings in this book are based on the average price of a three-course dinner without drinks:

£ under 30TL   ££ 30–60TL   £££ over 60TL

black and strong coffee (*kahve*) in tiny cups, Turkish wines of reasonable quality, Turkey's own Efes Pilsen beer and anise-flavoured *rakı*, which turns cloudy like absinthe when water is added.

Lunch is usually eaten between 12.00 and 14.00 and most restaurants open from around 11.00. Some will close around 15.00 and then open again in the evening, but most stay open all day. A tip of 10 per cent is normal and expected except in informal eateries of the self-service kind. Credit cards are generally accepted in most restaurants; look for the logos on the window or by the till.

Doluca (D) and Kavaklıdere (K) are the two best-known Turkish wine estates. Çankaya (K) is a decent blend of four different grape

⬤ *Traditional Turkish meze fare*

varieties, as is the Villa Doluca red. Moskado (D) is from aromatic grapes, Kavak (K) is a standard, light white for fish, and Ancyra (K) is a fruity and aromatic red. Sarafin (D) is a stronger red. Both estates produce sparkling wines.

Picnic meals can be enjoyed during non-winter months in any of the city's parks and there is no shortage of small supermarkets and corner shops selling provisions. Fresh bread is best bought in the morning; look out for the street carts selling fresh *simit*, a ring-shaped savoury bread with sesame seeds. Fruit and vegetables are abundant except in winter, and there are many cheeses and dried meats to consider.

Where to go for a meal depends partly on what kind of experience you are seeking. For top-drawer dining with fine food from around the world – French or Japanese, perhaps – and discerning wine lists, the five-star hotels in the Taksim area (see page 100) should not disappoint. If you prefer to go for Turkish and international food, a rooftop terrace view of the Bosphorus and a romantic atmosphere, there are plenty of choices in the Beyoğlu (see pages 28 & 100), Karaköy (see page 88) or Ortaköy (see pages 102 & 113) areas. Sultanahmet (see page 60) has its own crop of rooftop restaurants, many of which are remarkably affordable when you throw in stunning after-dark vistas of the Blue Mosque (see page 64) and Aya Sofya (see page 64). Stylish, design-conscious restaurants are more likely to be found around Taksim and Beyoğlu than Sultanahmet or Galata.

The traditional Turkish restaurant is the *lokanta*, and it usually serves pre-cooked food, which is kept warm in steel display tins. Menus may not be in English but you can just point at what you'd like to try, take a risk, and be surprised; vegetarians can choose the obvious non-meat dishes and rice. Equally traditional are the meat-

based kebab joints, *kebapçı* or *ocakbaşı*, and *pide* restaurants that
serve a flat bread base with various toppings.

USEFUL DINING PHRASES

I would like a table for ... people
... kişilik bir masa istiyorum
... kishilik beer masa istiyourum

May I have the bill, please?
Hesap, lütfen?
Hesap, lewtfen?

Waiter/Waitress!
Garson!
Garson!

Could I have it well cooked/medium/rare, please?
İyice kızartılmış/normal/az pişmiş olsun lütfen?
Iyidje kezartelmesh/normal/az pishmish olsun lewtfen?

I am a vegetarian. Does this contain meat?
Ben vejeteryenım. Bu yiyecek et içeriyor mu?
Ben vejeteryen-aem. Boo yee-yecek et ee-cher-ee-yor moo?

Where is the toilet (restroom)?
Tuvalet nerede acaba?
Tuvalet nerede adjaba?

I would like a cup of/two cups of/another coffee/tea
Bir fincan/iki fincan/bir fincan daha kahve/çay istiyorum
Beer findjan/eki findjan/beer findjan daha kahve/chai istiyourum

Entertainment & nightlife

The Romans and Ottomans knew all about indulging the senses and having a good time and a new generation of young Istanbulites have created a lively and gregarious nightlife of their own. There are two neighbourhoods to know about and the one that is easier to reach if staying in Sultanahmet (see page 60) is Beyoğlu, around Galata and down the side streets off İstiklal Caddesi. Here, tucked away in narrow lanes, are smoky jazz clubs, chill-out bars and rooftop haunts where young professionals share a bottle of wine while gazing down at the twinkling lights of vessels in the Bosphorus darkness. The other area kicks into gear with the arrival of warm days in June and, sharing the understandable obsession for sea views, hugs the shoreline at Ortaköy (see pages 102 & 113). The scene is alfresco and more designer-conscious than Beyoğlu; the mood is Mediterranean but the wine and *rakı* is pure Turkish. Less socially mixed than Beyoğlu, the air of affluence in Ortaköy is unmistakable.

In Sultanahmet itself the entertainment scene is more visitor oriented and along Divan Yolu Caddesi, where hostels draw in backpackers, there is a string of pubs where the music pulsates

WHAT'S ON?

Every two months, *The Guide Istanbul* (5TL in bookshops and newsstands, but look for free copies in hotels, cafés and restaurants) has listings of the new bars and hottest clubs and restaurants in town, as well as details of current exhibitions in the art galleries.

◆ *Rooftop cafés are among the favourite sites for chill-out moments*

until the early hours of the morning. Shows featuring Turkish belly dancing are usually as tacky as they sound and a good sing-along at a sociable restaurant like Kır Evi (see page 70) can be more enjoyable. It's also fun to take in one of the intriguing whirling dervish performances advertised on billboards and posters. Tickets for these can usually be bought at short notice.

April's International Istanbul Film Festival (see page 10) is testimony to the city's interest in films but at other times of the year, unless you speak Turkish, options are generally limited to Hollywood blockbusters and the occasional English success in their original language. It is always best to check at the box office when buying tickets, as some major releases may be dubbed into Turkish. There are plenty of cinemas, mostly around İstiklal Caddesi and Kadıköy, and seats should be booked in advance. Credit cards are accepted, and the average price is 10TL or less, with discounts sometimes for early screenings and for teachers or students (ID is not always required).

Theatre is nearly always in Turkish but the major cultural centres also host music, ballet and opera. Events featuring international orchestras are not uncommon. **Biletix** (❶ (0216) 556 9800 Ⓦ www.biletix.com) is a central booking system for many events, but often it is better to buy your ticket directly from the venue.

The **Atatürk Cultural Centre** (❶ (0212) 243 6923) in Taksim Square is a major venue and is home to the State Opera and Ballet, the Istanbul State Theatre Company and the **Istanbul State Symphony Orchestra** (Ⓦ www.idso.gov.tr). The box office is usually open 10.00–18.00. For details of other venues and events, check listings magazines or ask at the tourist office. The **Istanbul Foundation for Culture and Arts** (Ⓦ www.iksv.org) organises annual film, theatre and music festivals (see page 10).

⬥ *Whirling dervishes offer mystical dance entertainment*

Sport & relaxation

As European Capital of Sport 2012, Istanbul's sporting profile is currently higher than ever. The city is also bidding to host the 2020 Olympic Games.

SPECTATOR SPORTS
Football

The city's hands-down favourite sport is football, and it is not only the Bosphorus that divides Galatasaray, on the European side, from Fenerbahçe, over the water at Kadıköy. The rivalry is intense and, with Fenerbahçe claiming 25 million supporters across Turkey compared to Galatasaray's four or five million, a little one-sided. When either side achieves a notable victory, especially if chasing a European title, you will see and hear the crowds around Taksim Square. Tickets can be bought at either stadium in the week

● Beşiktaş supporters cheering on their team

preceding the game. There is a third Istanbul team, Beşiktaş, whose black-and-white colours contrast strongly with the yellow-and-blue of Fenerbahçe and the yellow-and-red of Galatasaray.

Beşiktaş İnönü Stadium ⓐ Spor Caddesi, Beşiktaş, close to Dolmabahçe Palace ⓣ (0212) 236 7201 ⓦ www.bjk.com.tr

Fenerbahçe Şükrü Saracoğlu Stadium ⓐ Kadıköy ⓣ (0216) 449 5667 ⓦ www.fenerbahce.org.tr

Galatasaray Ali Sami Yen Stadium ⓐ Mecidiyeköy ⓣ (0212) 216 1500 ⓦ www.galatasaray.org

PARTICIPATION SPORTS
Swimming

Five-star hotels have swimming pools, gyms and saunas, but some have a nasty habit of charging guests. If you want to swim, try the beaches in Büyükada on a visit to Princes' Islands – but don't dip so much as a toe in the polluted Bosphorus or the Golden Horn.

RELAXATION
Hamams

Istanbul's perfect antidote for tired limbs and tourist fatigue, and a cultural experience in its own right, is the *hamam*. A visit to a Turkish bath is up there with seeing the Topkapı Palace or the Blue Mosque, but a lot more soothing on the body. Men and women have their own sections, modesty is preserved with towels, and the process starts with a period of unwinding in a steam-filled hot room. There follow bouts of soaping and a vigorous exfoliating body scrub (a do-it-yourself ticket costs less but is also less fun), finished off with a body massage. The *hamam* experience is best enjoyed at the historic baths of Çemberlitaş (see page 60) or Cağaloğlu (see page 74), though a more private session is available at the Ambassador Hotel (see page 37).

Accommodation

You should not have a problem finding somewhere to stay in Istanbul, whatever your budget and tastes, although the best deals will be snapped up in summer and advance Internet booking is advisable. Use hotels' websites wherever possible. Other useful websites include ⓦ www.istanbul.com and, for reservations, ⓦ www.istanbulreservation.com. For hostels and the least expensive accommodation options, ⓦ www.hostelbookers.com is a good site. Please note that prices are sometimes quoted in euros.

Sultanahmet, the centre for sightseeing (see page 60), has a concentration of affordable accommodation, including hostels, plus some attractive hotels. Bus route TZK1 and tram line 1 serve this area. Across the Golden Horn in Beyoğlu (see page 28) you will find a selection of mid-range hotels and, because of the area's 19th-century history, there is some character to the place as well as easy access to İstiklal Caddesi and to Galata Bridge for Sultanahmet. Take bus TKB1, the funicular (Tünel) or the Nostalgia Tram to Tünel Square in Beyoğlu. At the top end of İstiklal Caddesi, in and around Taksim Square (see page 100), the top-notch, brand-name hotels cluster and provide five-star accommodation. Take bus TTK1, 70FE or 70KE, the Nostalgia Tram or the metro to Taksim Square.

PRICE CATEGORIES

Accommodation ratings in this book are based on the average price per person per night for a room in high season. Tax and breakfast are usually included. Out of season, rates may be lower.
£ under 90TL ££ 90–160TL £££ over 160TL

Hotels are categorised by the government using a one- to five-star rating and there is also another category for one-off 'Special' hotels, earnt as a result of the historic status of their buildings. This category does not reflect service or amenities, but room rates often match four- and five-star places even though the facilities may be restricted by preservation orders. What you do get is a unique experience, and advance booking is essential in high season.

Room rates, which usually include a buffet breakfast, tend to be seasonally adjusted and the higher rates apply to the April–October period and the Christmas/New Year break. Do not be timid about bargaining for a discount, especially if you are staying more than one night, and if a sea view is important, clarify this before confirming your booking. It is often the case, though not with five-star hotels, that a 10 per cent discount or more will be given if you pay in cash rather than by credit card. There is a hotel-booking desk at the airport but avoid this if you can because the rates are predatory.

All the hotels listed here are comfortable, well-run establishments and, apart from dorm beds in hostels, the rooms come with en-suite bathroom and air conditioning. Televisions are standard but only cable or satellite service provides English-language news programmes.

For hotels on the Asian side of the Bosphorus and on the Bosphorus coastline, see pages 129 and 139.

HOTELS

Gülşa £ Small rooms but clean and centrally located. No breakfast.
ⓐ İstiklal Caddesi, Acara Sokak 7, Galatasaray (Karaköy to Galatasaray)
ⓣ (0212) 251 6171 ⓔ hotelgulsa@mynet.com

Hanedan £–££ Same management as the Alp and Peninsula and an equally well-run establishment with its own roof terrace.

🅐 Akbıyık Caddesi, Adliye Sokak 3 (Sultanahmet) ❶ (0212) 516 4869
🆆 www.hanedanhotel.com

Peninsula £–££ Roof terrace, functional rooms but friendly management and airport pick-up for a small fee. 🅐 Akbıyık Caddesi, Adliye Sokak 6 (Sultanahmet) ❶ (0212) 458 6850 🆆 www.hotelpeninsula.com

Şebnem £–££ Family-run, friendly guesthouse with small but tasteful rooms and superb sea views from the rooftop. 🅐 Akbıyık Caddesi, Adliye Sokak 1 (Sultanahmet) ❶ (0212) 517 6623 🆆 www.sebnemhotel.net

Alp ££ Smart-looking hotel, well run, with safety boxes, cable TV and a fridge to keep your drinks in before bringing them up to the rooftop bar for views of the Bosphorus. 🅐 Akbıyık Caddesi, Adliye Sokak 4 (Sultanahmet) ❶ (0212) 517 7067 🆆 www.alpguesthouse.com

Ayasofya ££ Comfortable, faded elegance; not to be confused with the more expensive Ayasofya Pansiyonları. 🅐 Küçük Ayasofya Caddesi, Demirci Reşit Sokak 28 (Sultanahmet) ❶ (0212) 516 9446 🆆 www.ayasofyahotel.com

Grand Hotel de Londres (Hotel Büyük Londra) ££ This hotel is quite central and has been in service since 1881. Despite various renovations, the hotel still clings to the atmosphere of the 1900s. 🅐 Meşrutiyet Caddesi 117 (Karaköy to Galatasaray) ❶ (0212) 245 0670 🆆 www.londrahotel.net

Hotel Amira ££ Close to the sights with a roof terrace overlooking the Sea of Marmara. 🅐 Mustafa Paşa Sokak 79, Küçük Ayasofya Mahallesi (Sultanahmet) ❶ (0212) 516 1640 🆆 www.hotelamira.com

Ambassador £££ Great location (and has a *hamam*). Direct bookings
include airport pick-up and breakfast on the rooftop terrace.
🅐 Ticarethane Sokak 19 (Sultanahmet) ❶ (0212) 511 9828
🆆 www.hotelambassador.com

Anemon Galata £££ Next to the Galata Tower, this Special category
hotel has a terrace café and gloriously classical décor. 🅐 Büyük
Hendek Caddesi 5, Bereketzade Mahallesi (Karaköy to Galatasaray)
❶ (0212) 293 2343 🆆 www.anemonhotels.com

Ayasofya Pansiyonları £££ Ottoman-style boutique hotel with
Special status in a picturesque location next to Topkapı Palace.
🅐 Soğuk Çeşme Sokak (Sultanahmet) ❶ (0212) 513 3660
🆆 www.ayasofyapensions.com

Galata Residence Camono Apart Hotel £££ This hotel offers large
rooms with kitchens (and therefore no breakfast), and an authentic
sense of living in old Istanbul. 🅐 Bankalar Caddesi, Felek Sokak 2,
Galata (Karaköy to Galatasaray) ❶ (0212) 252 6062 🆆 www.galata
residencehotel.com

Lush Hip Hotel £££ This modern hotel is located in one of the most
lively spots around Taksim and offers a wide spectrum of services
to its customers. 🅐 Sıraselviler Caddesi 12, Taksim (Taksim Square
& beyond) ❶ (0212) 243 9595 🆆 www.lushhotel.com

The Marmara Istanbul £££ Landmark hotel with grand views,
five-star service and a busy atmosphere; confirm whether breakfast is
included when booking. 🅐 Taksim Square (Taksim Square & beyond)
❶ (0212) 251 4696 🆆 www.themarmarahotels.com

Pera Palace £££ Museum-like hotel where Agatha Christie stayed and wrote *Murder on the Orient Express* in room 411. ❸ Meşrutiyet

⬤ *The Sarnıç Hotel in Sultanahmet*

Caddesi 52 (Karaköy to Galatasaray) ☎ (0212) 377 4000
ⓦ www.perapalace.com

Point Hotel £££ Nearly 200 rooms, Wi-Fi and DVD players in the rooms, plus views of the Bosphorus. ➋ Topçu Caddesi, Taksim Square (Taksim Square & beyond) ☎ (0212) 313 5000
ⓦ www.pointhotel.com

Richmond £££ In the heart of the city, with sea or city views and good eating possibilities. ➋ İstiklal Caddesi 227 (Karaköy to Galatasaray)
☎ (0212) 252 5460 ⓦ www.richmondhotels.com.tr

Sarnıç Hotel £££ Boutique-ish feel to this 16-room hotel, with rooftop breakfast and good restaurant. ➋ Küçük Ayasofya Caddesi 26 (Sultanahmet) ☎ (0212) 518 2323 ⓦ www.sarnichotel.com

Swissôtel The Bosphorus £££ Stylish, five-star hotel with excellent facilities. Close to Taksim Square but awkward to reach on foot; easy with taxis. ➋ Bayıldım Caddesi 2 (Taksim Square & beyond)
☎ (0212) 326 1100 ⓦ www.swissotel.com

HOSTELS
Istanbul Hostel £ Not as noisy as some of the nearby hostels, with a pleasant atmosphere, rooftop terrace and downstairs bar. ➋ Kutlugün Sokak 35 (Sultanahmet) ☎ (0212) 516 9380
ⓦ www.istanbulhostel.net

Sultan Hostel £–££ Dorms and singles, slightly dearer doubles, café, outdoor bar with good views. Free use of Internet. ➋ Akbıyık Caddesi 21 (Sultanahmet) ☎ (0212) 516 9260 ⓦ www.sultanhostel.com

THE BEST OF ISTANBUL

Istanbul is so awash with cultural treasures and apparently must-see sights that a first-time visitor can feel overwhelmed. It's a good idea to work out your priorities; if you become enamoured with the city there will always be a return trip. Ticking off visits to postcard sights will exhaust you, and you will probably have a more enjoyable time if you take it easy, find some time to wander and allow for Turkish serendipity.

TOP 10 ATTRACTIONS

- **Mosques** Not all of them, but the Blue Mosque (see page 64) and Süleymaniye Camii (see page 78) are two of the most impressive and beautiful.

- **Topkapı Palace & Harem** Principal residence and pleasure palace of the Ottoman sultans (see pages 63 & 66).

- **Aya Sofya** Former church, former mosque, huge of dome and monumentally fascinating (see page 64).

- **Pummelling pleasures at a *hamam*** Tension and fatigue scrubbed and massaged away in an ancient steam bath. The best are Çemberlitaş (see page 60) and Cağaloğlu (see page 74).

- **Cruising the Bosphorus** Straddle Europe and Asia with a trip up the Bosphorus (see page 116).

- **Buzzing bazaars** The hyper-real Spice Bazaar and, if you want a bazaar experience on a mega scale, the Grand Bazaar as well (see page 76).

- **Jazzy moments at the Nardis Jazz Club** Enjoy every permutation of the genre at this fabulous, legendary club (see page 99).

- **Afternoon tea at Pera Palace Hotel** Time travel to the 1890s and get your antioxidants in style (see page 90).

- **Cocktails over the Bosphorus** Get sloshed in one of the many rooftop terrace restaurants in Beyoğlu and blame it on the intoxicating view (see page 28).

- **The Istanbul Modern & the Pera Museum** Contemporary art at the city's hottest galleries (see pages 93 & 94).

🔽 *The Grand Bazaar in Istanbul*

Suggested itineraries

HALF-DAY: ISTANBUL IN A HURRY

It would be a mad rush to see both sides of the Golden Horn (see page 76); by staying in Sultanahmet you can explore this historic site and enjoy a walk beginning at the Blue Mosque (see page 64). Even a quick visit inside will reveal its splendour and the same could be done for nearby Aya Sofya (see page 64), best reached by walking through Arasta Bazaar for some shopping on the hoof. From here it is five minutes to a tram stop on Divan Yolu Caddesi – cafés, restaurants and bars here offer refreshment – buy a ticket at

● *Enjoy a stop at Aya Sofya fountain park after a visit to the Blue Mosque*

the booth and hop on a tram for a short ride to Eminönü. Here you will see the Golden Horn and sense the majesty of the city and, if there is still time, pop into the nearby Spice Bazaar (see page 76) for some oriental razzmatazz.

1 DAY: TIME TO SEE A LITTLE MORE

The half-day itinerary above could easily stretch into a day's activity just by slowing down the pace. The extra time would also allow for a Turkish bath at Çemberlitaş (see page 60) before boarding a tram to Eminönü. Alternatively, instead of a *hamam*, the Galata Bridge can be crossed on foot, by tram or taxi, or take your lunch at one of the many restaurants underneath it while gazing at the busy sea traffic. There might still be time to take in the Istanbul Modern (see page 93), five minutes by taxi from the other side of Galata Bridge.

2–3 DAYS: TIME TO SEE MUCH MORE

The first day, or day and a half, could be occupied with the suggestions above, while the extra time would allow for a visit to Topkapı Palace (see page 66) and its harem, some leisurely shopping in the byways off İstiklal Caddesi and/or a trip up the Bosphorus. There would also be time to think about after-dark entertainment by way of a rooftop restaurant overlooking the Bosphorus, a bar or club to unwind in or, in summer, a taxi out to Ortaköy (see pages 102 & 113) for one of the chic, waterside restaurants.

LONGER: ENJOYING ISTANBUL TO THE FULL

Once you have enjoyed all of the above, you will have time to experience the full Top 10 (see page 40). Save the Turkish bath until last – you will really appreciate it!

Something for nothing

Sultanahmet's cityscape at night is there for the taking and the lit-up exteriors of the Blue Mosque (see page 64) and Aya Sofya (see page 64) are an experience in themselves. Even a very small donation will cover a visit to the Blue Mosque. No one minds if you wander into the period-piece Pera Palace Hotel (see page 90), pretending you have just stepped off the Orient Express, or, with the famous train in mind, visit the free Orient Express museum (see page 78) at the railway station. Every Thursday, 10.00–14.00, entrance to the Istanbul Modern (see page 93) is free.

For the small price of a ticket on the ferry (2TL each way), an evening could be enjoyed by taking one of the regular boats from Eminönü to Kadıköy (see page 130). Along the way you will experience the splendour of the Bosphorus and the city at night. Disembarking at Kadıköy you set foot in Asia and the atmosphere can be soaked up on a short walk before catching a boat back.

Beyoğlu and Taksim are full of temptations for your credit card but walk for free into Çukurcuma by going down Sıraselviler Caddesi from Taksim Square. Five minutes down this road, follow the signs pointing right to Galatasaray and Karaköy. You enter Ağa Hamamı and follow the next sign to Galatasaray by turning right at the Or-Ka store, then take the first left downhill, passing Evihan and Leyla (see page 108). Follow the street down, turn left and take the first right at the Ottoman shop and then left again. The street is full of little galleries and the architecture of old Istanbul. At the bottom, go left into Hayriye Caddesi and follow it around. Walk through the entrance to French Street and its restaurants on your right and up the steps at the other end. Turn left here and then right onto Yeni Çarşı Caddesi with its bookshops, one of which has an inexpensive downstairs café. This street leads on to İstiklal Caddesi and a right turn returns you to Taksim Square.

Also lending itself particularly well to a pleasant walk is the area around the Edirne Gate (Edirnekapi) in the northern city walls. Take in the exquisite minaret of the Mihrimah Sultan Camii mosque, the charming exterior of the Kariye Camii (St Saviour in Chora) church and the impressive three-storey façade of the Tekfur Sarayi (Palace of the Porphyrogenitus), a ruin dating to the 13th century.

⬤ *Explore the Bosphorus by ferry as the sun sets*

When it rains

Nine of the Top 10 attractions are not dependent on fine weather; only the enjoyment of a cruise up the Bosphorus relies on a fine day. The Blue Mosque (see page 64) and Süleymaniye Camii (see page 78), as well as Aya Sofya (see page 64), need to be appreciated from the outside, especially after dark, but once inside you are protected from the elements. The rooms of Topkapı Palace (see page 66) and the harem tour are all weather-proof and many hours could be spent wandering the covered Grand Bazaar (see page 76). A wet day is the ideal time to benefit from a Turkish bath because you can spend as much time as you like in the steam room and linger restfully over a drink after the experience before leaving the *hamam*.

Two historically important attractions that would make a Top 12 list are the Basilica Cistern (see page 63) and Dolmabahçe Palace (see page 105), and both these places are impervious to the weather. Museums, of course, are ideal places when it rains and the Archaeological Museum (see page 63) and the adjoining Museum of the Ancient Orient (see page 63) could easily occupy half a day. There are also a number of smaller museums that might not grab your attention when the sun shines but are worthy of your time if the subject matter appeals. Strong contenders are the Museum of Turkish and Islamic Arts (see page 66) and the Military Museum (see page 104), and not to be forgotten is the small Orient Express museum at the railway station (see page 78). The station has the atmospheric Orient Express restaurant and a café extension on to one of the platforms, and there is a period charm to enjoy while sipping a drink and watching the railway traffic.

By way of entertainment, the cinemas of Istanbul are a means of escaping the rain and, before or after, a leisurely drink and/or meal is always to be had in one or more of the numerous cafés, bars or restaurants in Beyoğlu (see page 28) or around Taksim (see page 100), the areas where most of the cinemas are located. Spending longer than you might otherwise have planned in a café or bar is a great way to find yourself chatting to Istanbulites and enjoying their company.

🔺 *Keep dry at the Orient Express museum*

On arrival

TIME DIFFERENCE

Istanbul is on Eastern European Time (EET), which is two hours ahead of Greenwich Mean Time (GMT). Between the end of March and the end of October, clocks are put forward by one hour for daylight saving.

ARRIVING

By air

Atatürk International Airport (❶ (0212) 465 3000 ⓦ www.ataturk airport.com) is 23 km (14 miles) west of Sultanahmet and has all the facilities you would expect, including ATMs, a 24-hour tourist information office and a left luggage facility.

The Havaş airport bus departs from outside the arrivals hall every half-hour from 04.00 to 21.00 and at regular intervals from 21.00 to 01.00, and takes about 45 minutes to reach Taksim Square. A one-way ticket costs 10TL. The return bus departs from outside the Havaş ticket office on Cumhuriyet Caddesi, just off Taksim Square, every half-hour between 04.00 and 23.30.

To reach Sultanahmet, either get off the Havaş bus at Aksaray and take a taxi or tram, or take the metro from the airport to Zeytinburnu. From here, you can transfer to a tram straight into Sultanahmet. Taxis to Taksim, Sultanahmet and other destinations are available from outside the arrivals hall.

Another arrival point for planes is **Sabiha Gökçen Airport** (❶ (0216) 585 5000 ⓦ www.sgairport.com) in Pendik on the Anatolian side of Istanbul, 40 km (25 miles) from Kadıköy. Havaş buses between Taksim Square and the airport run every hour between 04.00 and 01.00.

By rail

Long-distance trains from Europe arrive at Sirkeci Railway Station (see page 77), in the heart of the city, next to Eminönü, and tram and bus stops for Sultanahmet and Taksim Square.

By road

Nothing is gained by driving in Istanbul; the traffic is dense and parking spaces are extremely scarce in this city that is so easy to get around by foot, taxi and, to a lesser extent, public transport.

⬥ *Istanbul is two hours ahead of Greenwich Mean Time (GMT)*

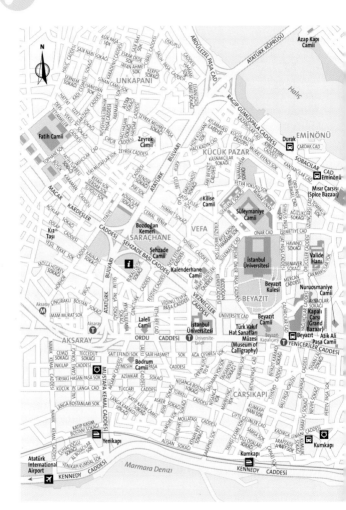

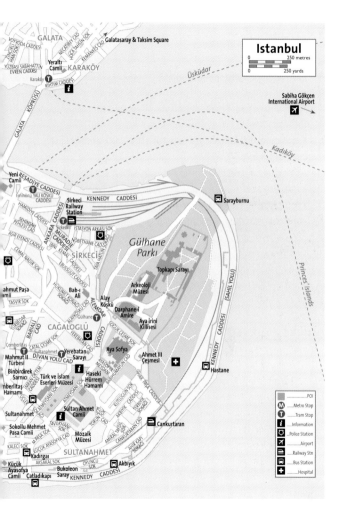

Istanbul

0 ───── 250 metres
0 ───── 250 yards

GALATA

VOYVODA CADDESI

HANCERLI SOK

NECATIBEY CAD

HOCA TAHSIN SOK

KEMANKES CAD Galatasaray & Taksim Square

YÜZBASI SABAHATTIN
EVREN CADDESI

Yeraltı
Camii   KARAKÖY

Karaköy 🚊

RIHTIM CADDESI

Üsküdar

Sabiha Gökçen
International Airport ✈

GALATA KÖPRÜSÜ

Kadıköy

Yeni
Camii   RESADIYE CADDESI

Eminönü YALI KÖSKÜ
CADDESI

Sirkeci
Railway
Station

KENNEDY   CADDESI

Sarayburnu

HAMIDIYE CADDESI

ANKARA CADDESI

SEHINSAH
PEHLEVI CAD

MURADIYE CADDESI

IBNI KEMAL CADDESI

Sirkeci 🚊

ISTASYON ARKASI SOK

NÖBETHANE CAD

TAYA HATUN SOK

AŞIR EFENDI CADDESI

CEMAL NADIR SOK

SIRKECI

Gülhane
Parkı

Topkapı Sarayı

Princes' Islands

ahmut Paşa
amii

HOCODET CADDESI

Bab-ı
Ali

ALEMDAR

Alay
Köşkü

ALAYKÖSKÜ CAD

Arkeoloji
Müzesi

TASVIR SOK

BABIALI CAD

CAĞALOĞLU

Gülhane 🚊

Darphane-i
Amire

SOĞUK ÇESME SOK

Aya İrini
Kilisesi

Çemberlitaş 🚊

ÇATAL ÇESME SOK

Mahmut II
Türbesi

Sultanahmet 🚊

DIVAN YOLU CAD

Yerebatan
Sarayı

KENNEDY   CADDESI (SAHIL YOLU)

DIVAN YOLU CADDESI

Aya Sofya

Ahmet III
Çeşmesi

Hastane ✚

Binbirdirek
Sarnıcı

Türk ve İslam
Eserleri Müzesi

Haseki
Hürrem
Hamamı

nberlitaş
Hamamı

Sultanahmet

🚌

YERABATAN CADDESI

KUTLUGUN SOK

Sultan Ahmet
Camii

TAVUKHANE SOK

Cankurtaran

🚌

Sokollu Mehmet
Pasa Camii

KÜÇÜK AYASOFYA CAD

Mozaik
Müzesi

SULTANAHMET

AKBIYIK CADDESI

CANKURTARAN SOK

AMIRAL TAFDIL SOK

KALECI SOK

Küçük
Ayasofya
Camii

Kadırgaı

AKSAKAL SOK

Çatladıkapı

Bukoleon
Saray

OYUNCU
SOK

Akbıyık

🚌

KENNEDY   CADDESI

Legend:

- ◾ ......POI
- Ⓜ ......Metro Stop
- 🚊 ......Tram Stop
- ℹ️ ......Information
- 🏢 ......Police Station
- ✈ ......Airport
- 🚆 ......Railway Stn
- 🚌 ......Bus Station
- ✚ ......Hospital

IF YOU GET LOST, TRY ...

Excuse me, do you speak English?
Affedersiniz, İngilizce biliyor musunuz?
Afeadehrseeneez, ingilizh'dje biliyour musunuz?

**Excuse me, is this the right way to ... the tourist office/
the old town?**
Affedersiniz, ... 'e/a/ye/ya buradan mı gidilir ... turist enformasyon
bürosu/eski şehir?
*Afeadehrseeneez, ... e/a/ye/ya buradan me gidilir ... tourist
enformasyon buerosu/eski shehir?*

Can you point to it on my map?
Haritamın üzerinde gösterebilir misiniz?
Haritamaen uezerinde goesterebilir misiniz?

FINDING YOUR FEET

Istanbul can be a confusing place when first setting out to travel
across the city, but it takes only a short while to learn the ropes.
If you're from the UK, watch out when crossing roads as they drive
on the right here. Wherever you come from, beware of vehicular
traffic because indicators are infrequently used and pedestrian
rights are a fanciful notion for many drivers. In fact, even when the
traffic lights are green for you, do not start crossing the road until
you are sure that all cars have stopped. Although Istanbul is quite
safe, you should be aware of the possibility of pickpockets in
crowded areas.

⬥ Hop on the Nostalgia Tram for a ride in modern Istanbul

ORIENTATION

Istanbul is divided by a narrow strait of water, the Bosphorus, which also divides Europe from Asia and this creates a European and an Asian half of the city. The Golden Horn is an inlet of water that feeds into the Bosphorus from the European side, and this divides European Istanbul itself into two areas: Sultanahmet (see page 60), the old city where most of the historic sites are to be found, and the more modern metropolis centred around İstiklal Caddesi and Taksim Square (see page 100). While most of your sightseeing time will be spent in and around Sultanahmet, it is the other side of the Golden Horn that boasts a concentration of restaurants, bars and clubs.

The Galata Bridge is the most usual route you will use for crossing between Sultanahmet and Taksim (see page 76). From the Taksim side of the bridge, the Tünel funicular railway will take you in seconds uphill to Beyoğlu (see pages 28 & 100). This is the elegant 19th-century quarter of European Istanbul and its main boulevard, İstiklal Caddesi, runs up to Taksim Square.

Beyond Taksim, to the northeast and on the shore of the Bosphorus, are the neighbourhoods of Beşiktaş (see page 100) and Ortaköy (see pages 102 & 113). These areas have attractions of their own and a host of entertainment possibilities by way of drinking, eating and clubbing.

Across the Bosphorus, on the Asian side of Istanbul, the main centres where you are likely to spend time are Kadıköy and Üsküdar (see page 130).

GETTING AROUND

Despite there being a system that encompasses funicular and catamaran alongside the more usual modes of public transport,

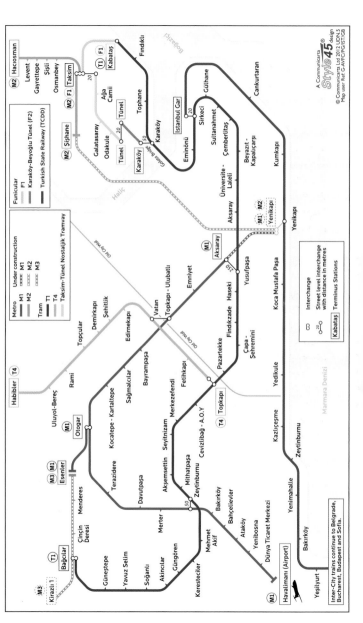

MAKING THE MOST OF ISTANBUL

THE AKBIL TRAVEL PASS

The Akbil system saves time and some money if you are staying for more than a few days and decide to use public transport. It uses a metal tag, accepted electronically on trams, buses, funicular railway and metro, and is bought at main stations (including Zeytinburnu if you are coming from the airport). You can also benefit from free transfers from one mode of transport to another, provided you get on the new vehicle within the hour. There is a refundable deposit for the metal tag and its value can be updated as and when it becomes necessary.

99 per cent of the time it's better – and more enjoyable – to walk. It's easy to travel between most of the principal attractions on foot. Topkapı Palace (see page 66), Aya Sofya (see page 64) and the Blue Mosque (see page 64) – the three major sights – are conveniently close to one another, and other significant places, like the Basilica Cistern (see page 63), Grand Bazaar (see page 76) and the Çemberlitaş *hamam* (see page 60) are just a short walk away.

Istanbul has a good and efficient tram system that connects with the metro. There is a flat rate fare, making it excellent value. There are ambitious plans to extend the metro to the Asia side and provide better connections with Sabiha Gökçen Airport, in readiness for the 2020 Olympic bid.

The bus system is efficiently run by **IETT** (see Ⓦ www.iett.gov.tr for full timetable and route information) and is very cheap. Payment must be made before boarding; tickets can bought either from the official white booths found close to the major bus stations such as Taksim and Eminönü, or, for a small mark-up, from most local

newsagents. Akbil tokens are accepted as well, see box opposite.
The destination is displayed electronically on the front of the bus.

The old funicular railway (known as the Tünel) climbs the steep
uphill journey of 500 m (550 yds) from Karaköy to Tünel Square in
Beyoğlu, the start/end of İstiklal Caddesi. A newer super-fast funicular,
F1, travels from Kabataş up the steep hill to Taksim every five minutes.

Licensed taxis, bright yellow in colour and relatively inexpensive,
are everywhere and can be hailed on the street. Fares are digitally
metered, with meters starting at 2.5TL and then clocking up 1.4TL for
every kilometre travelled. There is no difference between daytime
and night-time rates. The bridge toll will be added to your fare if

⬥ View of the Topkapı Palace with boats on the river

crossing one of the Bosphorus bridges. Tipping is not expected, although rounding up the fare to the nearest lira is common.

Boats travel constantly up and down the Bosphorus and across it to Kadıköy and Üsküdar. The principal terminus is at Eminönü. Boats also depart from Karaköy, just across the Galata Bridge and opposite Eminönü (but not for the Bosphorus cruises). All piers are clearly marked with their destinations and you purchase your ticket from the nearby booths. Boats to Kadıköy and Üsküdar cost just over 1.5TL and a single ticket for travel up the Bosphorus is between 13 and 20TL, depending on the time you travel. Catamarans also run on the traditional boat lines, but they have separate piers and their timetable can be quite different. Schedules of all boats and catamarans can be obtained by visiting the English version of Ⓦ www.ido.com.tr

The new metro system is still under construction and although some lines are in operation they are of little use to visitors. They generally serve the suburbs and do not access Istanbul's main attractions.

Ⓞ *Light up your day with a visit to a craft shop*

THE CITY OF
Istanbul

Sultanahmet

Sultanahmet is small and compact, relatively traffic-free compared to the rest of the city and an area you can easily find your way around on foot. As you walk around, be prepared for some persistent, if polite, carpet-shop touts along the way.

SIGHTS & ATTRACTIONS

Baths of Roxelana
This two-domed structure was built in the mid-15th century as the baths for worshippers at nearby Aya Sofya and named after the wife of the sultan, Süleyman the Magnificent, under whose orders it was built. The building was a government-run carpet and *kilim* shop for some time, but there are plans to reopen it as baths. ❸ Aya Sofya Square 4 ❶ (0212) 638 0035 ❶ 08.00–24.00

Çemberlitaş
Known also as Constantine's Column, this elegant porphyry column was brought from Egypt in AD 330 as part of the city's new status as the capital of the Byzantine Empire. It has been restored a number of times, most recently in 2006, though no one is thinking of re-topping it with a replacement statue of the emperor that originally adorned its summit. The column is open to view, beside the entrance to the historic Çemberlitaş *hamam*; go on, take a peep and decide – can you leave Istanbul without taking a bath? ❸ Vezir Hanı Caddesi 8

Çemberlitaş Hamamı
One of Istanbul's most historic Turkish baths, dating back to the 16th century. Prices range from 40TL for a bath and a do-it-yourself

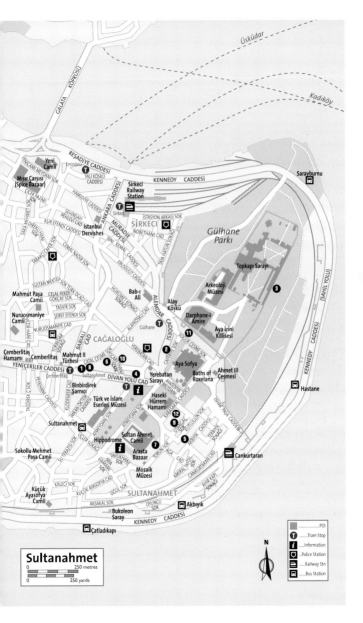

Sultanahmet

0	250 metres
0	250 yards

Üsküdar

Kadıköy

GALATA KÖPRÜSÜ

REŞADİYE CADDESİ

Eminönü

Yeni Camii

Mısır Çarşısı (Spice Bazaar)

BALIKÇILAR MEYDANI SOK

KENNEDY CADDESİ

YALI KÖŞKÜ CADDESİ

HAMIDIYE CADDESİ

ANKARA CADDESİ

Sirkeci Railway Station

İSTASYON ARKASI SOK

Sarayburnu

FATIH CADDESİ

TAHMIS CADDESİ

SALI PAZARI

SALA MEHMET SOK

KEHINSAL PEHLEVI CAD

AŞİR EFENDİ CADDESİ

CEMAL NADIR SOK

İstanbul Dervishes

MURADIYE CADDESİ

İBNI KEMAL CADDESİ

EBUSSUT CADDESİ

SİRKECİ

Sirkeci

NOBETHANE CAD

TAYA HATUN SOKAĞI

Gülhane Parkı

Topkapı Sarayı

❸

KENNEDY CADDESİ (SAHİL YOLU)

TABAK CAD SOK

SULTAN MEKTEP SOK

TÜRK OCAĞI CAD

CELAL FERDİ GÖKÇAY SOK

HÜKÜMET KONAĞI SOKAĞI

ALAYKÖŞKÜ CAD

Bab-ı Ali

ALEMDAR CADDESİ

Alay Köşkü

Arkeoloji Müzesi

Darphane-i Amire

❶❶

Aya İrini Kilisesi

Mahmut Paşa Camii

TASVIR SOK

ŞEREF EFENDİ SOK

Nuruosmaniye Camii

NURUOSMANIYE CAD

CAĞALOĞLU

YEREBATAN CAD

❷

SOĞUK ÇEŞME SOK

Gülhane

TURBEDAR SOK

BABIALI CAD

ÇATAL ÇEŞME SOK

CABIGAN CAD

ÇEŞMELI SOK

Aya Sofya

ÇEŞME SOK

Çemberlitaş Hamamı

Çemberlitaş

Mahmut II Türbesi

❶❽

❶ Çemberlitaş

Sultanahmet

DİVAN YOLU CAD

❹

Yerebatan Sarayı

AYASOFYA MEYDANI

Baths of Roxelana

Ahmet III Çeşmesi

YENİÇERİLER CADDESİ

KLODFARER CAD

Binbirdirek Sarnıcı

❶ i

Türk ve İslam Eserleri Müzesi

Haseki Hürrem Hamamı

❶❷

KABASAKAL CADDESİ

Hastane

KIÇ SOK

PEYKHANE CADDESİ

KLODFARER CADDESİ

İMRAN ÖKTEM CAD

ÜÇLER SOKAĞI

Sultanahmet

ATMEYDANI SOK

Hippodrome

Sultan Ahmet Camii

❼

Arasta Bazaar

❺

İSHAK PAŞA CADDESİ

TEVKIFHANE SOK

TERBIYIK SOKAĞI

KUTLUGUN SOK

UTANGAC SOK

MISTIK SOK

Sokollu Mehmet Paşa Camii

ŞEHİT MEHMET PAŞA SOK

KALECI SOK

KÜÇÜK AYASOFYA CAD

OĞUL SOK

Mozaik Müzesi

TORUN SOK

KAPIÇIHANE SOK

NAKILBENT SOK

AMIRAL TAFDIL SOK

CANKURTARAN CAD

Cankurtaran

Küçük Ayasofya Camii

AKSAKAL SOK

SULTANAHMET

OYUNCU SOK

Bukoleon Saray

KENNEDY CADDESİ

Akbıyık

AHIR KAPI SOKAĞI

Çatladıkapı

N

	POI
T	Tram Stop
i	Information
	Police Station
	Railway Stn
	Bus Station

scrub, to 60TL for a bath and massage, or 100TL for the full works.
ⓐ Vezir Hanı Caddesi 8, off Çemberlitaş ☎ (0212) 522 7974
ⓦ www.cemberlitashamami.com.tr ⏱ 06.00–24.00
ⓘ Admission charge

Gülhane Parkı (Gülhane Park)

Once the sultans' private palace park, this area of green offers welcome relief from the hustle and bustle in and around the palace. As well as offering a picnic site in the shade, there is a tea garden and, if you walk northeast and cross Kennedy Caddesi, a viewing point for the meeting of the Golden Horn and the Bosphorus. You will need to retrace your steps to leave the park on to Alemdar Caddesi and the Gülhane stop on the tram line.

Hippodrome (Sultanahmet Square)

Imagine massed crowds rising to their feet in Byzantium's greatest stadium as rival chariot teams gallop towards the finishing line... The Hippodrome, known as Sultanahmet Square and open to the public 24 hours, gives you a sense of grand, linear space – the stadium was enlarged by Constantine to hold as many as 100,000 people.

There are some suitably ancient monuments at the southwest end of the square. The Egyptian Obelisk, dated 1500 BC, stands next to the 5th-century Serpentine Column from the Temple of Apollo at Delphi – both were shipped in by Constantine. The third, dilapidated-looking monument on the site has an unknown provenance. At the northern end of the Hippodrome lies the Basilica Cistern (see opposite). The Blue Mosque and Museum of Turkish and Islamic Arts are also located here, and the square is close to tourist information points.

Outside Topkapı Sarayı (Topkapı Palace)

At the corner of Babi-I Hümayun Caddesi and Soğuk Çeşme Sokak stands the early 18th-century Fountain of Ahmet III (Ahmet III Çeşmeşi), a suitably elegant approach to the picturesque Soğuk Çeşme Sokak and its traditional painted houses. To enter the first courtyard of the palace, walk through the Imperial Gate in front of the fountain, passing the 6th-century Byzantine church of Haghia Eirene (which was never converted into a mosque). The twin-towered entrance to the palace is straight ahead.

Yerebatan Sarayı (Basilica Cistern)

Close to where Alemdar Caddesi meets Yerebatan Caddesi is the entrance to the largest underground cistern in the city, the Basilica Cistern, built to supply water for the palace area under Justinian in AD 532. The roof is held up by 12 rows of 28 columns, with each column over 8 m (26 ft) high. Two of the columns rest on bases that are shaped into Medusa heads. ❸ Yerebatan Caddesi 1 ❶ (0212) 522 1259 ❶ 09.00–18.30 (summer); 09.00–17.30 (winter) ❶ Admission charge

CULTURE

Arkeoloji Müzesi (Archaeological Museum & Museum of the Ancient Orient)

Between them, these two museums, covered by one entrance ticket, contain a large collection of works of art and artefacts from ancient Greece and Rome as well as priceless treasures from pre-classical civilisations. There is far too much to list here, but try not to miss the carved marble tomb depicting Persian forces being defeated by Alexander the Great, the world's earliest surviving peace treaty (1269 BC) providing for the mutual release of political prisoners, and

the animal relief from the time of Nebuchadnezzar in Babylon.
🅐 Osman Hamdi Bey Yokuşu, Gülhane ☎ (0212) 520 7740
🕒 09.00–17.00 Tues–Sun ❶ Admission charge

Aya Sofya (St Sophia)

The 'Church of Holy Wisdom', also known by its Greek name, Haghia Sophia, was built by Emperor Justinian in the 6th century AD and after 916 years was converted into a mosque after the Ottomans conquered the city. In 1935 it was converted into a museum – so no arguments over its theological identity – while its world significance remains undisputed in terms of monumental architecture. The dome measures 30 m (33 yds) in diameter and is supported by 40 brick-built ribs that depend on four colossal pillars for their stability. Apart from the remarkably absorbing silence of the vast, domed space, there are fine mosaics and marbles which are not easily seen in the poor light. 🅐 Aya Sofya Square ☎ (0212) 528 4500 🕒 09.00–17.30 ❶ Admission charge

Sultan Ahmet Camii (Blue Mosque)

Taking its name from the characteristically blue *İznik* tiles that decorate the interior, the famous Blue Mosque can prove more soul-stirring from the outside, especially at night when it is lit up and shines serenely with a strange self-possession. Built in the early 17th century, the construction plans aroused controversy because it was apparently thought that a mosque with six minarets would sacrilegiously challenge the supremacy of the mosque at Mecca. The interior is flooded with natural light. There is a free sound and light show from May to September from 19.30 outside the mosque.
🅐 Hippodrome ☎ (0212) 518 1330 🕒 08.30–19.00 (closed during prayer times) ❶ No shorts; women must cover their hair (veils provided)

◐ *The many beautiful windows of Aya Sofya*

Topkapı Sarayı (Topkapı Palace)

The numero uno visitor attraction, a been-there-and-bought-the-T-shirt kind of place, Topkapı Palace is undeniably difficult to resist and especially so when you have to enter it to access the harem. The palace was the administrative and erotic centre for the rulers of the Ottoman Empire from 1465 to 1853 and there is a lot to see in one visit; you may want to just pick out some of the highlights and reserve some energy and interest for the tour of the harem. The treasury is as full of glittering riches as you would expect and includes the emerald-decorated Topkapı Dagger, featured in the Peter Ustinov classic *Topkapı*, and the Spoonmaker's Diamond which, if you believe the blarney, was bought for three spoons from a junk merchant. The Circumcision Room has a most attractive exterior of *İznik* tiles from the 16th and 17th centuries. Before you leave the palace, seek out the last building built in the complex; it is now the Konyalı Café (see page 69), and even if you don't eat or drink, the panoramic views from the terrace are worth admiring.
ⓐ Soğuk Çeşme Sokak ⓣ (0212) 512 0480 ⓛ 09.00–19.00 Wed–Mon (summer); 09.00–17.00 Wed–Mon (winter) (last entry 1 hr before closing) ❶ Admission charge

Türk ve İslam Eserleri Müzesi (Museum of Turkish & Islamic Arts)

An excellent space with a collection of Islamic works of art housed in a graceful old Ottoman residence restored in 1843, the museum has survived largely unaltered into the 21st century. The exhibits you'll find here are richly varied: Persian miniatures, Turkish carpets, works of highly wrought calligraphy, paintings and ethnographic displays. There is a nice little shop, too, for cards and small mats.
ⓐ Hippodrome ⓣ (0212) 518 1805 ⓛ 09.00–19.00 Tues–Sun (summer); 09.00–17.00 Tues–Sun (winter). ❶ Admission charge

TOPKAPI HAREM

The first stop on the mandatory tour is the Court of the Black Eunuchs, the harem's guards, before proceeding to the luxurious rooms of the *valide* sultan (see page 12). As you continue, some of the many highlights include the decorous dining room of the fruit-and-floral-loving Ahmet III and the over-the-top sumptuous luxury of Murat III's chamber. It is up to you to imagine the debauchery and licence indulged in by the sultans, although the sober fact is that the harem was the living quarters for a sizeable community of people and not – well, not always – the venue for decadent orgies. That was what the Romans did. ❸ Topkapı Palace, Soğuk Çeşme Sokak Ⓦ www.topkapipalace.com ● 09.00–17.00 Wed–Mon; guided tours every 30 mins 09.30–16.00 ❶ Crowds can be very heavy, with long queues, so go early or late if you can; separate admission charge at the entrance of Topkapı Palace

RETAIL THERAPY

Ahmet Yesevi Vakfı Within a former Islamic monastery, discover a traditional handicrafts centre, bookshop, gift shop and café in a flower-filled garden. ❷ Küçük Ayasofya Camii Avlusu, Cankurtaran Mahallesi ❶ (0212) 638 5012 ● 08.00–23.00

Les Arts Turcs A must-see in Sultanahmet for anyone curious about Turkish culture. The centre sells the works of many local artists, including paintings, ceramics, glassware, jewellery and clothing. There are frequent cultural activities and workshops. ❷ İncili

Çavuş Sokak 37, 3rd floor, Alemdar Mahallesi ☎ (0212) 527 6859
🌐 www.lesartsturcs.com 🕙 09.30–19.00 Mon–Sat

Galeri Cengiz One of the many small shops in Arasta Bazaar,
parallel to the Hippodrome but behind the Blue Mosque, selling
embroidered bags, shoes and boots using materials from Uzbekistan
and Turkmenistan. 📍 Arasta Bazaar 157 ☎ (0212) 518 8882
🕙 09.00–22.00 (summer); 09.00–20.30 (winter)

Gift Land Easy to find, situated on one of Sultanahmet's main visitor-
oriented streets full of restaurants and bars, and unpretentiously
offering just what the shop's name suggests. Come here for
ceramics, paintings, carpets and, well, gifts. 📍 Akbıyık Caddesi 51
☎ (0212) 518 4434 🕙 09.00–23.00

İznik Classics Quality ceramics with prices that start at around 25TL
for small items and go up to 400TL. The proprietor has two other
shops in the vicinity and you may find yourself being persuaded to
make a visit, but there is no compulsion to buy anything. 📍 Arasta
Bazaar 67 ☎ (0212) 517 1705 🌐 www.iznikclassics.com 🕙 09.00–21.00
(summer); 09.30–17.30 (winter)

Nakkas Fine Rugs Housing an amazing collection of 20,000 rugs, this
shop was built above a 6th-century Byzantine cistern and is used as
space for contemporary art. 📍 Kaleici Sokak, Nakilbent Sokak 33
☎ (0212) 516 5222 🌐 www.nakkasrug.com 🕙 09.00–21.30

Trust Leather A long-standing leather store selling their own designs
and custom-made clothes and accessories. 📍 Küçük Ayasofya Caddesi
8 ☎ (0212) 458 5343 🕙 09.00–20.00

TAKING A BREAK

Anatolian House £ ❶ A cosy, small eatery off busy Divan Yolu
Caddesi that offers welcome relief after a morning's schlepping
around the sights. Stuffed aubergines, rice in rolled grape leaves,
Turkish ravioli, varied drinks with and without alcohol. ❸ Divan Yolu
Caddesi, Hoca Rüstem Sokak 7 ❶ (0212) 512 3920 ❶ 08.00–24.00

Caferağa Medresesi £ ❷ The perfect resting place for a drink or light
lunch after visiting nearby Topkapı Palace is a peaceful courtyard with
tables, serving meatballs, salad, pastries, coffee or a hot milk with
orchid root. While you are here check out the one-day handicraft
courses that take place in what used to be the study rooms of an
old college and the teachers' work that's for sale. ❸ Caferiye Sokak
❶ (0212) 513 3601 ❿ www.tkhv.org ❶ 08.30–19.00

Konyalı Café £ ❸ The only place to eat inside Topkapı Palace, and if
you use the cafeteria service the prices are very reasonable considering
the location and the marvellous views of the Sea of Marmara and
the Golden Horn from the terrace or glassed-in pavilion. The
restaurant itself is not exorbitant and is well worth it if you want to
linger. Eat early or late to avoid the worst of the crowds. If you just
need a tea or coffee and a *simit* (sesame-topped bread ring), there
is a kiosk near the ticket desk for the harem. ❸ Topkapı Palace
❶ (0212) 513 9696 ❿ www.konyalilokantasi.com ❶ 08.30–19.00
Wed–Mon (summer); 08.30–17.00 Wed–Mon (winter)

Sultan Ahmet Köftecisi £ ❹ Justly famous *köfte* (meatball) eatery,
established in the 1920s, which has queues forming outside as
sunset approaches during Ramadan. Make sure you are eating in

the restaurant with the brown façade because other restaurants using the same name have set up in the same street. ⓐ Divan Yolu Caddesi 12 ⓣ (0212) 520 0566 ⓦ www.sultanahmetkoftesi.com ⓛ 10.30–23.00

AFTER DARK

RESTAURANTS

Albura Kathisma ££ ❺ This traditional *meyhane* (tavern), set above a maze of tunnels, was once part of the Byzantine senate. ⓐ Akbıyık Caddesi 26 ⓣ (0212) 638 4428 ⓛ 10.00–23.30

Ambassador ££ ❻ A neat little rooftop terrace with skyline views of the Blue Mosque and Aya Sofya. A weekly barbecue in the summer, vegetarians catered for and fresh fish from the local market if ordered in advance. Alternatively, come here late just for drinks and the vista. ⓐ Ticarethane Sokak 19 ⓣ (0212) 512 0002 ⓦ www.hotelambassador.com ⓛ 12.00–01.00

Café Meşale ££ ❼ As it's in the heart of touristy Sultanahmet, few locals eat or drink here, but it is a fun place at night when there is always some live music and singing. You can dine or drink inside or at tables under the night sky in the forecourt area. ⓐ Arasta Bazaar 45 ⓣ (0212) 518 9562 ⓛ 09.30–01.00

Kır Evi ££ ❽ There are many after-dark possibilities in and around this area but Kır Evi wins hands down; cool atmosphere, candlelight, live music at night, friendly service and good-value meals. ⓐ Divan Yolu Caddesi, Hoca Rüstem Sokak 9 ⓣ (0212) 512 6942 ⓦ www.kirevi.com ⓛ 11.00–24.00

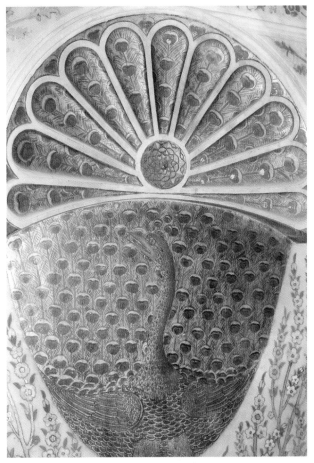

Peacock amid carnations from a 16th-century tiled kiosk

Rami Restaurant ££ ❾ This Ottoman-style, wood-slatted house, named after the Turkish painter whose works are on display, serves Ottoman dishes in an elegant and romantic setting. As usual, tables on the rooftop terrace need a reservation; it's worth the effort, as you will be rewarded with a grand view of the nightly Blue Mosque sound and light show. ⓐ Utangaç Sokak 6 ⓣ (0212) 517 6593 ⓦ www.ramirestaurant.com ⓛ 12.00–23.00

Rumeli Café ££ ❿ A cosy brick-walled café-restaurant set over two floors, which serves a menu of Turkish and Ottoman specialities as well as steaks. ⓐ Ticarethane Sokak 8 ⓣ (0212) 512 0008 ⓛ 11.00–23.00

Sarnıç Restaurant £££ ⓫ When the need for the rooftop dining fling is out of your system it is time to go deep underground and descend into a cavernous, millennium-old cistern and relish a dark, candlelit atmosphere. The food is so-so and the wine list pricey, but what a location for an evening out. ⓐ Soğuk Çeşme Sokak ⓣ (0212) 512 4291 ⓦ www.sarnicrestaurant.com ⓛ 19.00–23.00 (mid-Aug–mid-July)

Yeşil Ev £££ ⓬ Alfresco dining in a delightful garden setting with Aya Sofya as the backdrop, or inside a glasshouse with a floral motif. Kebabs, chicken curry and salads plus hot and cold appetisers. ⓐ Kabasakal Caddesi 5 ⓣ (0212) 517 6785 ⓦ www.istanbulyesilev.com ⓛ 12.00–23.00

BARS & PUBS
Cheers A popular pub that attracts backpacking budget travellers from the nearby hostels. There are two more like-minded pubs a few doors down. ⓐ Akbıyık Caddesi 20 ⓣ (0212) 526 0200 ⓛ 13.00–02.00

Sultan Pub An upmarket tourist trap in some respects but the outdoor tables make for a comfortable pre- or after-dinner drink; the cocktails are pricey. There is plenty of food of the pizza-burger-pasta kind. ❸ Divan Yolu Caddesi 2 ❶ (0212) 528 1719 ⓦ www.sultanpub.com.tr ⏱ 09.00–01.00

◑ *Restaurants beckon after dark*

Grand Bazaar & surrounds

The Grand Bazaar and its surrounding area is not as compact as Sultanahmet but the tram system serves as a point of reference as well as the means of getting to and from here. It runs past the Grand Bazaar at the Beyazıt stop and continues eastwards, stopping at Sultanahmet and two other stops before reaching Eminönü. At Eminönü there is the Galata Bridge crossing the Golden Horn to Karaköy and the funicular railway that zips you up to the start of İstiklal Caddesi. The sights and attractions of this section can all be reached on foot.

SIGHTS & ATTRACTIONS

Beyazıt Square
The square is a busy transport junction filled with buses and taxis. The military-style building you see to the north of the square is the entrance to Istanbul University but any sense of student life is drowned out by the traffic and crowds of people. Beyazıt Tower, inside the grounds of the university, can be climbed to the top for views over the city. In the square itself stands the grimy Beyazıt Mosque, the oldest surviving mosque in the city, inspired by Aya Sofya and providing a model that would be improved upon with the Süleymaniye Mosque.

Cağaloğlu Hamamı
A beautifully Baroque, 18th-century *hamam* and, yes, it has been used for film sets (one of the Indiana Jones escapades). As with Çemberlitaş Hamamı (see page 60), there is a choice of treatments, from the basic DIY job to the luxury massage. ⓐ Prof Kazım İsmail Caddesi, Cağaloğlu ⓣ (0212) 522 2424 ⓦ www.cagalogluhamami.com.tr ⓛ 08.00–22.00 (men); 08.00–20.00 (women) ⓘ Admission charge

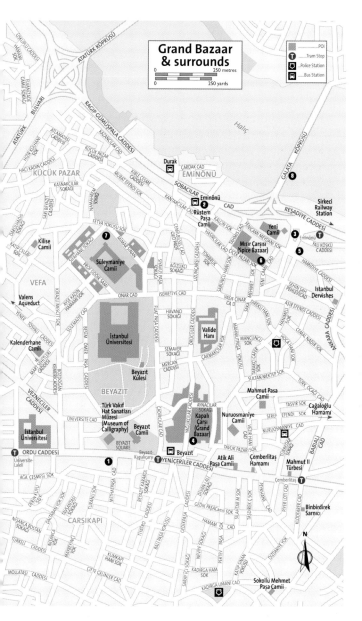

Haliç (Golden Horn) & Galata Köprüsü (Galata Bridge)

One of the great sights in Istanbul is the Golden Horn, the never-empty Galata Bridge spanning it, and the constant flow of traffic on the water. The ancient Greeks spotted its potential in the 7th century BC and it has been growing in importance ever since. It has also grown richer if you believe the story behind the name: the Byzantines threw so many riches into it when the Ottomans attacked that the surface sparkled with gold. It still sparkles at night with the twinkling lights of boats and ferries and walking across it at dusk and pausing in the middle to take in the whole scene offers a stirring sight of the great city. The bridge is underslung with fish restaurants and on a summer's evening it pays to linger here, if only for a drink or two.

Kapalı Çarşı (Grand Bazaar)

Like it or loathe it, the Grand Bazaar, or Kapalı Çarşı, is an experience you won't forget. To some it is full of character and imbued with an ambience wherein you can lose yourself, literally and figuratively; to others the place is a claustrophobic den where predatory merchants appear out of nowhere and where nothing can be bought without endless haggling. It probably depends on your mood, but see it you should; it is a fascinating, veritable labyrinth of streets with some 4,000 shops, including restaurants and cafés. There are some signposts but you will almost certainly lose yourself in the melée and exit at a different point from your entrance. ⓐ Kapalı Çarşı ⓦ www.kapalicarsi.org.tr ⓛ 08.30–19.00 Mon–Sat ⓘ Avoid Saturday, when it becomes just too crowded to enjoy.

Mısır Çarşısı (Spice Bazaar)

It is a matter of temperament, perhaps, if you prefer the Spice Bazaar to the Grand Bazaar, but if you want your senses played on in a minor

THE ORIENT EXPRESS

On its maiden run in 1889 the Orient Express chugged out of Paris and steamed 2,900 km (1,800 miles) in three days before pulling into its Istanbul destination at Sirkeci Railway Station (see below). The station and the Pera Palace Hotel (see page 90) were built for the Orient Express and both places continue to evoke that bygone era – with the help of Agatha Christie's *Murder on the Orient Express*, Graham Greene's *Stamboul Express*, and half-a-dozen films. The last train from Paris pulled into Istanbul in 1977.

but exquisite key then this is the market to visit. Built in the late 17th century, it still evokes the Ottoman world even though the shops selling spices, the special merchandise of this bazaar brought up along the Golden Horn from all quarters of the Ottoman Middle East, are now matched in number by those bulging with souvenirs, handicrafts and dubious aphrodisiacs. Stop at the Bab-ı Hayat restaurant (see page 86) if you feel the need for a break but, unlike the Grand Bazaar, the Spice Bazaar is not big or crowded enough to drain all your energy. The Spice Bazaar's Turkish name is Mısır Çarşısı, meaning Egyptian Bazaar, since it was built using money from import duties on Egyptian goods. ⓐ Eminönü ⓑ 08.30–18.30 Mon–Sat

Sirkeci Railway Station

The traffic here is busy and distracting, but stroll around the station a couple of times to take in the details, and its architectural merits begin to stand out. Functionality combines with Byzantine and Ottoman stylistic features and inside there is a splendidly old-fashioned restaurant, an impressive waiting room and a small **museum** devoted to the Orient Express. There is also a tourist office. ⓐ İstasyon Caddesi, just behind Yeni Camii (New Mosque), beside the flower market ⓣ (0212) 527 0051

Valens Aqueduct

Named after the Roman emperor who had the aqueduct built in the 4th century to bring water into the city, it functioned as such well into the 19th century. Now it straddles a busy road and is distant from other attractions, but if you take the Havaş airport bus to or from Taksim Square, you will pass underneath the structure and get a good impression of its mighty size. ⓐ Atatürk Bulvarı

CULTURE

Rüstem Paşa Camii (Rüstem Paşa Mosque)

Within easy walking distance of the Spice Bazaar, this delightful, mid-16th-century mosque built by Mimar Sinan (see page 81) does not impose itself physically and it is only when you are inside that its cultural richness makes an impression. The quality of the *Iznik* tiles is unrivalled, especially on the galleries, and there are beautiful patterns and pictorial panels to admire, all clearly lit with the natural light flowing in through the multitude of windows. ⓐ Hasırcılar Caddesi ⓣ (0212) 526 7350 ⓛ 08.30–18.00 (but avoid visiting during Friday prayers)

Süleymaniye Camii (Süleymaniye Mosque)

Mimar Sinan, the best of the Ottoman architects, designed this mosque complex for Süleyman the Magnificent and what a superb building it still is. The unadorned interior is stunning and the sense

⬤ *Even today the Spice Bazaar evokes the Ottoman world*

◔ One of Yeni Camii's inspiring minarets

MIMAR SINAN

The great architect Mimar Sinan (c. 1491–1588) came from Anatolia but his talents were spotted at a young age and he was brought to study in Istanbul. He was working as an engineer when Süleyman the Magnificent promoted him to chief architect and the sultan was rewarded with plans for the Süleymaniye Mosque and Rüstem Paşa Mosque. These are certainly Mimar Sinan's finest achievements, but he designed well over a hundred mosques and many other buildings, including the Çemberlitaş Baths.

Mimar Sinan transformed architectural tradition. His innovative reorganisation of interior space was partly an attempt to represent the perfect God through the perfect geometrical figure, the circle. His passion for perfection extended not only to the mosque itself but to the social complex outside it.

of equilibrium created by the open space is founded on geometry: the height of the dome is precisely double its diameter. In the adjoining cemetery you can admire the impressive tomb of Süleyman, which shines with inlaid ceramic stars. Here, too, is the tomb of his all-powerful wife Roxelana. ❸ Prof Sıddık Sami Onar Caddesi ✆ (0212) 522 0298 🕐 09.00–17.30 (but avoid visiting during Friday prayers) ⓘ Donation requested

Türk Vakıf Hat Sanatları Müzesi (Museum of Calligraphy)

On the west side of Beyazıt Square, this small museum will reward your time only if you are predisposed to appreciating the fine art

of Ottoman calligraphy. The words themselves may mean nothing but the skilled precision of the calligrapher, akin to the achievement of the monks who inscribed Dublin's *Book of Kells*, takes on its own beauty. Some of the calligrapher's tools are also on display here, plus miniatures from the Ottoman period.
ⓐ Beyazıt Square ⓣ (0212) 527 5851 ⓛ 09.00–16.00 Tues–Sat
ⓘ Admission charge

Yeni Camii (New Mosque)

It is impossible to miss seeing this monumental mosque because it dominates the Eminönü neighbourhood and the view coming over the Galata Bridge from the other side of the Golden Horn. Completed in the mid 17th century and the last of the great Ottoman mosques, its exterior is its most prepossessing feature. The plaza outside has some seats and low stone walls where you can picnic (with the pigeons) on a fine day. ⓐ Yenicami Meydanı Sokak, Eminönü ⓣ (0212) 527 8505 ⓛ 08.00–18.30 (but avoid visiting during Friday prayers)

RETAIL THERAPY

Ali Muhiddin Hacı Bekir The very first shop selling *lokum* (Turkish delight) is located opposite Hafız Mustafa Şekerlemeleri (see page 86) near Sirkeci Railway Station. It originally opened in 1777 as royal confectioners serving the Ottoman palaces. The interior has been faithfully restored and the shop is now a registered protected site. Do pick up some *lokum* while you're there – they have hazelnut and pistachio flavours as well as plain. ⓐ Hamidiye Caddesi 83, Eminönü ⓣ (0212) 522 0666 ⓦ www.hacibekir.com.tr ⓛ 08.30–19.00 Mon–Fri, 09.00–20.00 Sat & Sun

APHRODISIAQUE
DES
SULTANS
MESİR MACUNU

FİYATLARIMIZA
KDV
DAHİLDİR.

○ Love potions and loofahs at the Spice Bazaar

Günhan Three floors of fabrics and a modest selection of jewellery in the heart of the Spice Bazaar. The prices of the pretty shawls vary according to the quality of the embroidery and some bargaining will be the order of the day. ➌ Mısır Caddesi 47, Spice Bazaar ➊ (0212) 522 3840 ➍ 09.00–19.00

M & K You will pass this shop on your left if approaching the Grand Bazaar along Tavuk Pazarı from the Çemberlitaş tram stop. Pop in for Iranian caviar, candyfloss, Turkish olive oil in tins, Turkish chocolate, or honey and honeycomb from all over the country. ➌ Tavuk Pazarı 37 ➊ (0212) 520 7063 ➍ 09.00–19.00 Mon–Sat

Muhlis Günbattı A specialist shop for *suzani* (hand-appliquéd fabric) from Turkey's eastern neighbours, Turkmenistan and Uzbekistan, and a choice selection of Ottoman kaftans and *kilims*. ➌ Perdahçılar Sokak 48, Grand Bazaar ➊ (0212) 511 6562 ➍ 09.00–17.00 Mon–Sat

Özer A handicraft shop in the Spice Bazaar, Özer retails embroidered silk, cotton, cashmere and jewellery, and downstairs there are decorative home textiles. An attractive store and no hard sell. ➌ Mısır Caddesi 82, Spice Bazaar ➊ (0212) 526 8079 ➍ 09.30–18.30 Mon–Sat

Şişko Osman This is a well-established carpet shop in the Grand Bazaar and the carpets, rugs and *kilims* are quality items. It's a good idea, however, to check the quality and price of similar items in the store's competitors in the Grand Bazaar, if only to be able to haggle more effectively. ➌ Zincirli Han Caddesi 15, Grand Bazaar ➊ (0212) 528 3548 ➎ www.siskoosman.com ➍ 09.00–18.30 Mon–Sat

TAKING A BREAK

Beyazıt Internet Café £ ❶ Facing Istanbul University to the north in Beyazıt Square, look behind you and the sign for this café is hard to miss. Tea, coffee and confectionery are for sale and pleasant window seats overlook the busy scene down on the street. Chessboards are also at hand. ⓐ Yeniçeriler Caddesi, Uluçay İşhanı 47, Beyazıt Square ⓣ (0212) 638 8337 ⓛ 09.00–23.00 Mon–Sat

Borsa £ ❷ Crossing Yalıköşkü Caddesi from the Golden Horn side by the pedestrian bridge, Borsa is tucked away behind the bottom of the steps. A lovely clean and modern *lokanta* (traditional Turkish restaurant), with a self-service counter, and an excellent choice of traditional Turkish dishes. *Rakı* and cappuccino also available. ⓐ Yalıköşkü Caddesi 62, Eminönü ⓣ (0212) 511 8079 ⓛ 11.00–21.00 Mon–Sat

Coffee World £ ❸ Standing in the open square next to the New Mosque, with the Golden Horn behind you, this pleasant alfresco café is in the top right corner of the square. Shaded from the heat and providing a restful spot after a visit to the Spice Bazaar, it offers a choice of good coffee and light snacks. ⓐ Asmaaltı Caddesi, Kızılhan Sokak 18, Eminönü ⓣ (0212) 520 0204 ⓛ 08.00–19.00 Mon–Sat

Fes Café £ ❹ This is one of the best-known cafés inside the Grand Bazaar and its boho décor (check the Philippe Starck-designed chairs) blends in perfectly with the location. If there are no vacant tables for the sage tea and carrot cake, the Sultan Café next door is just as good, or pop around the corner to the neon-lit Divan Café Pastanesi for cakes and cream with lower prices than the Fes.

🅐 Halıcılar Caddesi 62, Grand Bazaar 🅣 (0212) 528 1613
🅛 09.00–19.00 Mon–Sat

Hafız Mustafa Şekerlemeleri £ ❺ This is a busy part of town and, if you have just walked over the Galata Bridge, finding somewhere quiet for a cup of tea and a snack is not easy. Hafız Mustafa Şekerlemeleri looks from the outside like a standard cake and *lokum* (Turkish delight) deli, but climb the stairs at the back and you'll find a small eating area. 🅐 Hamidiye Caddesi 86, Eminönü 🅣 (0212) 513 3610 🅛 06.00–22.00

AFTER DARK

RESTAURANTS

Bab-ı Hayat ££ ❻ Within a restored Ottoman building, discover a boutique restaurant serving delicious Ottoman and Turkish cuisine. The hand-painted ceiling in the Kubbe Altı room is a replica of the ceiling of the tomb of Sultan Mehmet IV, and the Altın Yol room overlooks the Spice Bazaar. Book in advance. 🅐 Mısır Çarşısı Sultan Hamam Girişi, Yeni Camii Caddesi 39/47, Eminönü 🅣 (0212) 520 7878 🅦 www.babihayat.com 🅛 10.00–19.00 (until 24.00 for large-group reservations)

Dârüzziyafe ££ ❼ This restaurant boasts a stunning location inside the Süleymaniye social complex, one of the most impressive examples of Ottoman architecture in Istanbul. Come here to sample traditional Turkish cuisine, such as meatballs with filo pastry, along with fresh fruit juices and herbal teas. 🅐 Şifahane Sokaği 6, Eminönü (beside the Süleymaniye Mosque) 🅣 (0212) 511 8414 🅦 www.daruzziyafe.com.tr 🅛 12.00–23.00

⬤ Take a break from your sightseeing and enjoy some traditional Turkish sweets

On Numara ££ ❽ Under Galata Bridge you are spoilt for choice when it comes to seafood restaurants, and at On Numara you can pick from a variety of fishy options: bonito, bream, sea bass and calamari. Sit outside and enjoy the location, or stay inside for the air conditioning and comfort. ⓐ Galata Bridge 10, Eminönü ❶ (0212) 243 9892 Ⓦ www.onnumaracafe.com ⏰ 08.00–03.00

ENTERTAINMENT
Istanbul Dervishes This Sufi music concert and whirling dervishes ceremony is performed by a group from the Galata Mevlevihanesi. ⓐ Ankara Caddesi, Hocapaşa Hamamı Sokak 5–9, Sirkeci ❶ (0212) 458 8834 Ⓦ www.istanbuldervishes.com ⏰ 19.30–20.30 Mon, Wed, Fri & Sun ❶ Admission charge

Karaköy to Galatasaray

The sights in this area are listed in the order you will encounter them
if walking across the Galata Bridge from Eminönü into the old port
area of Karaköy, then to Galata where the Tünel funicular railway
whisks you up to İstiklal Caddesi, and halfway up the pedestrianised
street, as far as Galatasaray. This whole area on the other side of the
Golden Horn used to be called Pera and is rich in attractions, both
ancient and modern, and everywhere can be reached on foot.

SIGHTS & ATTRACTIONS

Church of SS Peter & Paul

The Dominican Brothers saw their own church converted to
a mosque so they moved to this location and established a new
base. The church you see today was built in the mid 19th century
and is entered through a courtyard – Ottoman regulations would
not allow a church façade to face the street directly – and you
may have to search to find the doorway. ③ Galata Kulesi Sokak 26
❶ (0212) 249 2385 ● 07.00–08.00 Mon–Fri, 15.30–17.30 Sat,
10.00–12.00 Sun; other times by appointment

Galata Kulesi (Galata Tower)

Built by the Genoans in 1348 and used as a watchtower, Galata
Tower has been restored a number of times and is now a solid
structure boasting some of the finest views of the city on a sunny
day. The restaurant and evening show that take place at the top
are, frankly, forgettable, but a drink can be enjoyed while taking
in the vista. ③ Galata Kulesi Sokak ❶ (0212) 293 8180
ⓦ www.galatatower.net ● 09.00–20.00 ❶ Admission charge

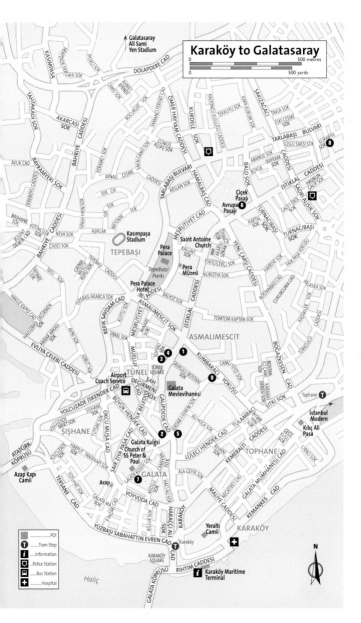

PERA

Pera, from the Greek for 'across' or 'beyond', became shorthand for the other side of the Golden Horn from Constantinople, now the areas of Galata and Beyoğlu. In time, and when Istanbul was the capital of Turkey, it became the European quarter of the city and foreign embassies (now just consulates) were established here, hence the tales of intrigue and spying that could give a dangerous edge to expatriate life in old Stamboul. At the same time, it became the shopping ground for affluent Europeans off the Orient Express.

Pera Palace Hotel

You can stay at this expensive institution (see page 38) or just wander in for refreshments in the *fin de siècle* patisserie or bar and soak up the atmosphere of this wonderfully unique hotel. Where other great hotels of the past, like Raffles in Singapore, have been manicured beyond recognition, the Pera Palace has remained virtually unchanged since it opened in 1892. There is a roll-call of famous guests, including Trotsky, Greta Garbo and Jackie Chan, on the wall near the antique lift, and in the bar there is a display cabinet relating a curious mystery about a key found in room 411, where Agatha Christie stayed. ❸ Meşrutiyet Caddesi 52, Tepebaşı ❶ (0212) 377 4000 Ⓦ www.perapalace.com

Avrupa Pasajı (Avrupa Passage)

Evocative of bourgeois Pera, the handsome but narrow, glass-roofed, marble-floored arcades that grace Istanbul can be walked past without being noticed. They are gems of urban architecture,

⬤ *Almost unchanged since 1892 – the patisserie at the Pera Palace Hotel*

modelled on Parisian arcades, and this one is filled with character.
🅐 Off Hamalbaşı Caddesi

Çiçek Pasajı (Çiçek Passage)

Another gorgeous arcade, this one is in the old Cité de Péra building
that was once an almost obligatory stop for the rich and fashionable
arriving in the city. Built in the 1870s, it fell into disrepair but has
been renovated and polished up rather nicely. There is a popular
eating complex at the back, and the adjoining fish market is certainly
worth a quick look.

⬥ *An architectural treasure on the street*

THE WHIRLING DERVISHES

Adherents of Sufism, a mystical branch of Islam, aspire to personal and ecstatic contact with the divine through dance, music and recitation. The best known of the various sects of Sufism are the Mevlevi, known as the whirling dervishes because of their fast, spinning dance, the *sema*, that aims for a trance-like communion with the spiritual realm of existence. The first dervishes were followers of the 13th-century Sufi guru Jelaleddin Rumi and also known as 'Mevlana', based in Konya, central Anatolia. The dancers who perform today are devotees of the sect, and the dance requires much practice and skill.

CULTURE

Galata Mevlevihanesi

This centre of Sufi culture, originally a monastery and now a small museum, is the venue for ceremonies of the famous whirling dervishes, the Mevlevi, most Sundays at 15.00 (phone in advance to make sure). Sufism was banned by the reforming Atatürk in the 1920s and this monastery survived only by turning itself into an educational institution. ❸ Galipdede Caddesi 15 ☎ (0212) 245 4141 🕐 09.00–17.00 Wed–Mon

İstanbul Modern (Istanbul Modern)

This is the epitome of contemporary Istanbul – artistic and dynamic, alive to the international arts scene but keen to make art accessible to all. A permanent exhibition of modern Turkish art, a large space for retrospectives and international exhibitions and a photography gallery all have their place here. Don't miss the entrance area, where trends in video and interactive works of art are showcased. Meclis-i-Mebusan Caddesi, Liman İşletmeleri Sahası Antrepo 4, Karaköy ❶ (0212) 334 7300 ❿ www.istanbulmodern.org ❶ 10.00–18.00 Tues, Wed & Fri–Sun, 10.00–20.00 Thur ❶ Admission charge (except 10.00–14.00 Thur when entry is free)

Pera Müzesi (Pera Museum)

The Istanbul Modern could have been a one-off, but the opening of the Pera Museum in 2005 confirmed Istanbul's status as the cultural capital of Turkey. The building itself is architecturally beautiful, built in the late 19th century but meticulously renovated to house four floors of exhibition space. Two levels are devoted to a permanent exhibition of Anatolian weights and measures and a collection of tiles and ceramics, but what will just as likely grab your attention are the international exhibitions (Henri Cartier-Bresson, for example) that the museum's private funds are capable of mounting. ❶ Meşrutiyet Caddesi 65, Tepebaşı ❶ (0212) 334 9900 ❿ www.peramuzesi.org.tr ❶ 10.00–19.00 Tues–Sat, 12.00–18.00 Sun

RETAIL THERAPY

Art Ena Down a side street, on your left off Galata Kulesi Sokak (which leads to Nardis Jazz Club and Galata House, see pages 99 & 98), this little shop and café retails jewellery, accessories and home-made tops and scarves. Try the gear on and then tuck into cheesecake, chocolate, sandwiches and coffee. ❶ Camekan Sokak 1, Kuledibi ❶ (0212) 243 5318 ❶ 09.00–21.00

◉ *A converted warehouse, setting the art agenda for Istanbul*

Artrium Turkish miniatures, calligraphy, paintings, cards, prints, film posters, ceramics and custom jewellery all mixed together; you'll feel as if you may unearth something priceless among all the stock. ⓐ Tünel Geçidi 7 ⓣ (0212) 251 4302 ⓛ 09.00–19.00 Mon–Sat

El Sanatları Evi Affordable hand-painted ceramics – plates, bowls, tea- and coffee-sets – and a reasonable choice. ⓐ İstiklal Caddesi 180A ⓣ (0212) 293 9990 ⓛ 10.00–21.00

Lale Müzik With an archive of nearly 8,000 jazz, ethnic and classical CDs, this is a paradise for music lovers. ⓐ Galipdede Caddesi 1 ⓣ (0212) 293 7739 ⓛ 09.00–19.30 Mon–Sat, 12.00–18.00 Sun

Pied de Poule Butik Retro clothes, accessories and furniture from the 1930s and '40s – to buy or just to hire. ⓐ Faik Paşa Yokuşu 19/1, Çukurcuma ⓣ (0212) 245 8116 ⓛ 12.00–18.30 Mon–Sat

Robinson Crusoe One of the best bookshops in the city for English-language publications, including books about Istanbul and Turkey and a good range of current magazines. ⓐ İstiklal Caddesi 389 ⓣ (0212) 293 6968 ⓛ 09.00–21.30 Mon–Sat, 10.00–21.30 Sun

TAKING A BREAK

Armada ££ ❶ A bright and clean eatery offering kebabs, *köfte* (meatballs) and other Turkish favourites. ⓐ İstiklal Caddesi 231B ⓣ (0212) 249 7927 ⓛ 11.00–21.30

Güney Restaurant ££ ❷ If you forsake the funicular and walk up to Galata from the bridge, you will need some refreshment and this

ARTY EATING

The über-smart restaurant at the Istanbul Modern (see page 93) is the ideal place for a drink and/or meal, not so much for the food but for a table by the large plate-glass window overlooking the sea. The chances are that a merchant vessel will be berthed just metres away behind the glass. Alternatively, there is a complex of less expensive eateries on your right as you approach the gallery after turning into it from Necatibey Caddesi.

old favourite does the business. No alcohol, but coffees and kebabs, mezes and chicken dishes. **a** Galipdede Caddesi, Kuledibi Şahkapısı Sokak 2 **t** (0212) 249 0393 **w** www.guneyrestaurant.com.tr **c** 07.30–23.00

KeVe ££–£££ ❸ Step out of the funicular railway at Tünel and this arcaded courtyard is immediately opposite. It tends to attract the self-conscious arty types with time on their hands, but retains its appeal as a calm and green oasis for tea, coffee or something stronger accompanying carrot cake or maybe figs marinated in cognac. **a** Tünel Square 6 **t** (0212) 251 4338 **w** www.kv.com.tr **c** 08.30–02.00

AFTER DARK

RESTAURANTS
Lokal £–££ ❹ This little eatery (no more than 20 people can be seated at any one time) is typical of the creative flair that makes this end of Beyoğlu such an exciting place on the contemporary food scene. The

menu is hard to pin down but there is a definite Thai edge to what is on offer. ⓐ İstiklal Caddesi, Müeyyet Sokak 9 ❶ (0212) 245 5744 ⓛ 12.00–03.00 Mon–Fri, 14.00–03.00 Sat

Venta Del Toro ££ ❺ Spanish cuisine in this airy and cheerful restaurant takes the form of tapas, toasted peppers, aubergine and goat's cheese, and quiche calamari, to name a few items. Turkish dishes and wines are on offer but Spanish wines also feature on the expansive drinks list. Live music Tues & Thur–Sat. ⓐ Galipdede Caddesi 95 ❶ (0212) 243 6049 ⓛ 10.00–03.00 (kitchen closes 24.00)

Barcelona Café & Patisserie ££–£££ ❻ Offering not only excellent cakes and pastries but great Mediterranean cuisine, this historic restaurant and patisserie is worth visiting simply in order to admire the fine architecture of the building. ⓐ İstiklal Caddesi 246, Asmalımescit Mahallesi, Beyoğlu ❶ (0212) 244 5459 ⓛ 07.00–24.00

Galata House ££–£££ ❼ Western powers at one stage had their own jurisdiction over their citizens' misdemeanours and this building was the British prison between 1904 and 1919. Complete with original cell door and prisoners' graffiti, this charming restaurant has tables in what was the tiny exercise yard, and live music at night. Indoor dining during the winter. ⓐ Galata Kulesi Sokak 15 ❶ (0212) 245 1861 ⓦ www.thegalatahouse.com ⓛ 12.00–24.00 Tues–Sun

Parsifal ££–£££ ❽ This small vegetarian restaurant is perfect for a quiet and intimate meal. The rich menu includes Balkan, Greek, Bulgarian and Jewish specialities. ⓐ İstiklal Caddesi, Akarsu Sokak 1, 2, 4, 5, Tomtom Mahallesi ❶ (0212) 245 2588 ⓦ www.parsifalde.com ⓛ 12.00–23.00

Leb-i Derya £££ ❾ Outstanding, wood-and-glass rooftop venue for after-dark drinks or a meal; take the lift up to the fifth level. Popular and therefore busy, consider coming also for brunch. Ottoman-style food and cool views. ⓐ Kumbaracı Yokuşu 57/7 ⓣ (0212) 293 4989 ⓦ www.lebiderya.com ⓛ 17.00–02.00 Mon–Thur, 17.00–03.00 Fri, 10.00–02.00 Sat & Sun

BARS & CLUBS

Babylon Premier live music club with the programme changing monthly and, every month, an Oldies but Goldies night for nostalgia-ravers. Book in advance for big events. Directly opposite the nightclub is a cosy little joint, appropriately named Little Wing, serving vegetarian food and Turkish herbal teas. ⓐ Seyhbender Sokak 3, Tünel ⓣ (0212) 292 7368 ⓦ www.babylon.com.tr ⓛ 21.00–24.00 Mon–Fri, 22.00–02.00 Sat & Sun (closed Mon & Sun if no events); ticket booth: 12.00–21.00 Tues–Sat

İndigo Come here for live performances of rock, indie and jazz music, parties and activities. ⓐ İstiklal Caddesi, Akarsu Sokak, Mısır Apt 1, 2, 4, 5 ⓣ (0212) 245 8567 ⓦ www.livingindigo.com ⓛ 20.30–24.00 Mon–Fri, 22.00–02.00 Sat & Sun

Nardis Jazz Club Live performances nightly in the city's best jazz club, named after a Miles Davis song. Ethnic, fusion, modern or classical – take what comes – and food too. ⓐ Galata Kulesi Sokak, Kuledibi Sokak 8 ⓣ (0212) 244 6327 ⓦ www.nardisjazz.com ⓛ 21.30–00.30 Mon–Thur, 22.30–01.30 Fri & Sat ⓘ Cover charge

Taksim Square & beyond

This area takes in the continuation of İstiklal Caddesi as far as Taksim Square, and encompasses the many imperial palaces and parks which lie dotted along the Bosphorus. Many of the bars and restaurants are tucked away in side streets off İstiklal Caddesi and around Taksim Square and can be easily reached on foot. The sights and cultural attractions are more spread out and buses and taxis are an option if you don't fancy a walk. The 40T bus service is a useful one, accessing Ortaköy and Beşiktaş. Dolmabahçe Palace and the Bosphorus waterfront can both be reached on foot from Taksim Square but the road network seems to have been designed exclusively for vehicles, meaning pedestrians are relegated to an inferior status. Returning from Ortaköy in the early hours of the morning is best done by taxi.

SIGHTS & ATTRACTIONS

Boho Galatasaray

This area of Beyoğlu, and the smaller neighbourhood of Çukurcuma within it (which is nicknamed the 'Soho of Istanbul') that lies between Sıraselviler Caddesi and İstiklal Caddesi, is a charming maze of quiet backstreets, best taken in by way of an unhurried stroll. It has become a cosmopolitan centre for small shops and miniature design emporiums, where you can happily while away hours rummaging delicately for authentic Ottoman fabrics and antiques (see 'Retail therapy', page 106). There are also many restaurants worth checking out along the way to consider returning to later for an evening meal. The area is an easy walk from Taksim Square.

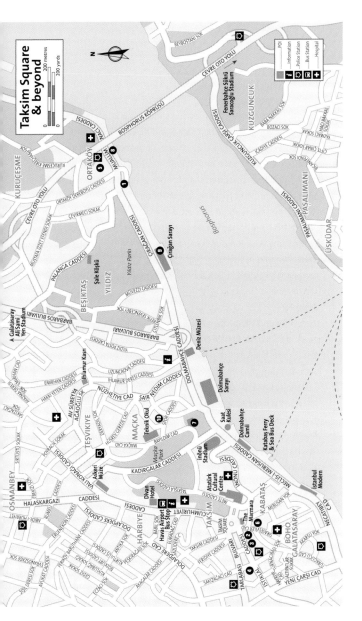

Çırağan Sarayı (Çırağan Palace)

Çırağan Palace was built as a comfort zone and sumptuous pad for Sultan Abdülmecid, but by the time it was completed in 1874, another sultan was on the throne and he was either murdered or committed suicide inside the palace. At one stage it also housed the Turkish parliament, until it was accidentally burnt down in 1910. Now it has been restored to its former glory and function and is once again providing luxury accommodation, though this time to anyone splashing out at the Çırağan Palace Kempinski Hotel (see page 112 for a night out at its Tuğra restaurant). Even if you opted not to blow your holiday budget on a room in the palace, you're free to wander in and have a look around. ⓐ Çırağan Caddesi 32 ⓣ (0212) 326 4646 ⓦ www.kempinski-istanbul.com ⓥ Bus: 40T

Ortaköy

Once a fishing village separated from the city, Ortaköy is now the most fashionable part of the long strip of outdoor bars, clubs and restaurants that stretches from Beşiktaş near Dolmabahçe Palace (see page 105). It jumps into high gear between April and autumn and at weekends attracts a high-octane crowd of Turkish revellers and jet-setters. It is theatrical and exuberant, perhaps a little too brash for its own good, but it serves as a dynamic reminder that there is more to Istanbul than Byzantine remains and ancient buildings. The quayside square is the epicentre of social life and here on the waterfront, amid all the razzmatazz, sits the solemn and stately Mecidiye Mosque, built in 1855 by the architect of Dolmabahçe Palace. ⓥ Bus: 40T

Taksim Square

The square is certainly not the prettiest sight in Istanbul, being a transport hub with forlorn patches of green struggling to

◯ *Taksim Square: a merry-go-round of vehicles at the heart of Istanbul*

survive, but this is the heart of modern Istanbul. As well as the bus service to and from Sultanahmet, the Havaş airport bus arrives and departs from Cumhuriyet Caddesi that runs north from the square.

Yıldız Parkı

A spacious green area punctuated with pavilions, small museums, villas and lakes, this park is ideal for a picnic. Much of what you see was put together under Sultan Abdülhamit II in the late 19th century and he chose to live here much of the time because he was worried that Dolmabahçe Palace might be attacked from the Bosphorus. The cultural highlight, and the most impressive building in the park, is the Şale Köşkü (Şale Pavilion, see page 106). There are places to drink and eat in the park but if you fancy some heavy-duty pampering in an opulent setting, then it is only a short walk to the Çırağan Palace Kempinski Hotel across the main road (see page 112). ⓐ Yıldız Parkı, Çırağan Caddesi ⓣ (0212) 261 8460 ⓛ 24 hrs (but access after 22.00 generally prohibited) ⓝ Bus: 40T, DT2

CULTURE

Askeri Müze (Military Museum)

The Military Museum can be reached on foot from Taksim Square in less than 20 minutes, or you can hop on any of the buses trundling up Cumhuriyet Caddesi from the square. The best reason for coming here is not so much to gawk at the cannons, weaponry and uniforms of the Ottoman period – the embroidered tents are well worth seeing – but to catch the marching band which plays outside from 15.00 every day that the museum is open. The rousing music comes from the Mehter Band, dating back to 1289 when it was composed of *janissaries* (infantry soldiers) who accompanied the

sultan into battle. ⓐ Vali Konağı Caddesi, Harbiye ⓘ (0212) 233 2720
ⓒ 09.00–17.00 Wed–Sun

Dolmabahçe Sarayı (Dolmabahçe Palace)

Situated on the Bosphorus waterfront, this was the residence
of the Ottoman sultans after it was built in the mid 19th century.
A Baroque pile of a place, its sheer theatricality and unashamed
luxury was an attempt by the Ottomans to reassert imperial
glamour at a time when the empire was in decline. There are two
sections, each covered by its own guided tour. If you are short of time,
take the Selamlık one because this takes in the magnificent
Ceremonial Hall, where your jaw will drop at the sight of the
chandelier (reputedly the heaviest in the world) and the gilt dripping
off everything around you. It's best to go early to avoid the queues
and beat the daily cap on visitors. ⓐ Dolmabahçe Caddesi, Beşiktaş
ⓘ (0212) 236 9000 ⓒ 09.00–16.00 Tues, Wed & Fri–Sun (summer);
09.00–15.00 Tues, Wed & Fri–Sun (winter) ⓘ Admission charge

Ihlamur Kasrı (Pavilion of the Linden Tree)

The Pavilion of the Linden Tree, another one-time residence of
pleasure-seeking sultans, is as pleasant as the name suggests;
a green oasis complete with fountains and flowering magnolias in
summer, but no trace of the linden (lime) trees that must have been
here at one time. There are two pavilions, designed by the architect
of Dolmabahçe Palace – and it shows – so if you enjoyed the palace
and wish to see more of the same, the Ihlamur Kasrı is worth a visit.
Guided tours are available, and there is a café in one of the pavilions.
ⓐ Ihlamur Teşvikiye Yolu, off Avukat Süreyya Ağaoğlu Sokak, Beşiktaş
ⓘ (0212) 259 5086 ⓒ 09.30–18.00 Tues–Sun (summer); 09.00–16.00
Tues, Wed & Fri–Sun (winter) ⓝ Bus: 40T ⓘ Admission charge

Şale Köşkü (Şale Pavilion)

The Şale Pavilion is at the top of the hill in Yıldız Parkı, but there is a road up to it and you can take a taxi if the climb does not appeal. The first section of the pavilion was modelled on a Swiss chalet, while the other two were specially designed to receive state visits from Kaiser Wilhelm II at the end of the 19th century. The guided tour is mandatory and points out that the large Hereke carpet you see was hand-knotted by 60 weavers and that part of a wall had to be knocked down to accommodate it. More eye-catching is the overall effect of the design that mixes Islamic with Baroque and rococo styles. You can decide for yourself if it works or not. ⓐ Yıldız Parkı, Beşiktaş ⓣ (0212) 259 4570 ⓛ 09.00–16.00 Tues, Wed & Fri–Sun ❶ Admission charge

RETAIL THERAPY

See page 44 ('Something for nothing') for walking directions that take in the Çukurcuma shops overleaf.

AvantGardeEast Near Galatasaray, this is one of the more diverting clothes shops on the main drag of İstiklal Caddesi. No designer-name outfits, but a creative selection of funky gear for anti-fashion dressing up. ⓐ İstiklal Caddesi, Galatasaray İş Hanı 120 ⓣ (0212) 245 1507 ⓛ 10.00–22.00

La Cave If you have come to realise that Turkey is producing some interesting wines, then this discriminating and knowledgeable wine store is worthy of a reconnaissance trip for that special bottle or two to bring home. ⓐ Sıraselviler Caddesi 109, Taksim ⓣ (0212) 243 2405 ⓦ www.lacavesarap.com ⓛ 10.00–21.00

Tradition meets beauty at Dolmabahçe Palace

Evihan Evihan's workshop for making glass beads is in the shop – it resembles Francis Bacon's studio – and this delightful Aladdin's cave retails unique jewellery, accessories, dresses and skirts that you will not find anywhere else. Men have to make do with a choice of cufflinks. ❸ Altıpatlar Sokak 8, Çukurcuma ❶ (0212) 244 0034 Ⓦ www.evihan.com ❶ 10.00–18.30 Mon–Sat

Leyla Not a single item of clothing in this shop is from the 20th century, never mind the present one, and you can look here for that special bed cover, pillow cover, jacket, scarf or hat. Quite an amazing little emporium. ❸ Altıpatlar Sokak 10, Çukurcuma ❶ (0212) 293 7410 ❶ 10.00–19.00 Mon–Sat

Mavi Jeans The jeans of choice for well-to-do Istanbulites below the age of 30. ❸ İstiklal Caddesi 123 ❶ (0212) 244 6255 ❶ 10.00–23.00

Mephisto Five levels of Turkish music, with everything from traditional folksy to New Age Sufi, plus the usual international big names. A café is on the premises. ❸ İstiklal Caddesi 125 ❶ (0212) 249 0687 Ⓦ www.mephisto.com.tr ❶ 10.00–24.00 Mon–Sat, 10.00–23.00 Sun

Retro AvantGardeEast Turkey's largest vintage and second-hand clothes shop, with around 30,000 items (including military uniforms and Turkish hats) and tailors on hand to tweak and repair clothes. ❸ İstiklal Caddesi, 166C Suriye Pasajı ❶ (0212) 245 6420 ❶ 10.00–23.00

Şamdan Antique Find Ottoman and Islamic art from the 19th century, along with more modern furniture and lamps. ❸ Altıpatlar Sokak 13A, Çukurcuma ❶ (0212) 245 4445 ❶ 09.30–18.30 Mon–Sat

△ Turkish wine makes for an interesting souvenir

Tombak II This little emporium of the old and ancient is facing you when you walk to the bottom of the street that Evihan and Leyla are on. It is stuffed with small antiques, jewellery, tin boxes from yesteryear, memorabilia, collectibles, and old suitcases, big and small, which could have come off the Orient Express. ❸ Faik Paşa Yokuşu 22A, Çukurcuma ❶ (0212) 244 3681 ● 10.00–19.00 Mon–Sat

TAKING A BREAK

Mado £ ❶ Two levels for ice cream, cakes and coffees at Ortaköy's smartest joint; grab a table by the window for views outside. ❷ Çırağan Caddesi, Osmanzade Sokak 16, Ortaköy ❶ (0212) 259 1015 ● 07.30–02.00

Hacı Baba ££ ❷ An old favourite with shoppers, almost as old as Hacı Abdullah (see below) but serving alcohol. The food is tasty and affordable and there is a terrace for outdoor meals in the shade. ❷ İstiklal Caddesi 39 ❶ (0212) 244 1886 ⓦ www.hacibabarest.com ● 11.30–24.00

Nature & Peace ££ ❸ One of the first restaurants in Istanbul to feature vegetarian meals and still one of the very few places where you can enjoy tofu-based dishes. ❷ İstiklal Caddesi, Büyükparmakkapı Sokak 15A ❶ (0212) 252 8609 ⓦ www.natureandpeace.com ● 10.00–05.00 Wed, Fri & Sat (DJ on these nights), 10.00–24.00 Sun–Tues & Thur

Hacı Abdullah ££–£££ ❹ Although this venerable establishment makes a strong claim to being the oldest still-functioning restaurant in the city, the feel of the place is remarkably contemporary. No alcohol, and Ottoman dishes all the way. It's worth a visit just to see the stained-glass dome above the mezzanine floor. ⓐ İstiklal Caddesi, Atıf Yılmaz Caddesi 9A ⓣ (0212) 293 0851 ⓦ www.haciabdullah. com.tr ⓛ 11.00–22.30

AFTER DARK

RESTAURANTS

Anjelique ££–£££ ❺ The bar and its martini menu are a big draw, plus there's the relaxed mood of the place and the scene looking out across the water. There is an evening menu of gourmet pizzas and excellent seafood. ⓐ Muallim Naci Caddesi, Salhane Sokak 10, Ortaköy ⓣ (0212) 327 2844 ⓦ www.istanbuldoors.com ⓛ 19.00–05.00 (summer); 22.00–05.00 Thur–Sat (winter)

Changa £££ ❻ Get in the mood with a special cocktail, satsuma *caipiroska* (vodka, tangerine and bergamot), and get down to the fusion-but-not-confusion menu. New Zealander Peter Gordon is the consultant chef so expect some surprises. A tasting menu for two is 100TL. The décor is a mix of Modernist art and the proto-industrial and, one claim to fame, a glass window set into the floor above the kitchen. ⓐ Sıraselviler Caddesi 47 ⓣ (0212) 251 7064 ⓦ www.changa-istanbul.com ⓛ 18.00–01.00 Mon–Sat (closes June–Sept)

Miyako £££ ❼ OK, it is a hotel restaurant, but this is the best place for satisfying those Japanese taste buds that other cuisines cannot reach. The set dinners include sushi, sashimi, tempura and teriyaki while the à la carte choices feature a sublime hot appetiser – seafood in motoyaki sauce – and some spicy seafood. ⓐ Swissôtel

The Bosphorus, Bayıldım Caddesi 2 ❶ (0212) 326 1100 Ⓦ www.
swissotel.com ❶ 19.00–23.00 Tues–Sun

Reina £££ ❾ The setting is everything – by the water under the
Bosphorus Bridge – and diners come here to be seen as much as to
enjoy the food. ❷ Muallim Naci Caddesi 44, Ortaköy ❶ (0212) 259 5919
Ⓦ www.reina.com.tr ❶ 19.30–04.00

Tuğra £££ ❾ Perhaps the ultimate in Bosphorus views, the setting
for an evening at the Tuğra is indeed magnificent and the terrace
beckons in summer. The food is Ottoman and there is live

⬥ *Çırağan Palace Kempinski Hotel has a majestic location right on the Bosphorus*

THE ORTAKÖY SCENE

Through the long summer nights, the waterside scene at Ortaköy pulsates with social life in the bars and restaurants that crowd the quayside and the cobbled byways that lead to more clubs and pubs in tiny ex-fishermen's cottages. Where you end up is likely to be decided by where you can find a table, so just wander about and see what comes up. Sipping a mojito while waiting for the sun to go down could make for a scene to remember.

traditional Turkish music. A place to spoil yourself. ⓐ Çırağan Palace Kempinski Hotel, Çırağan Caddesi 32 ① (0212) 326 4646 ⓦ www.kempinski-istanbul.com ① 19.00–23.00 Thur–Sun

Vogue £££ ⑩ The Mediterranean and Californian fusion dishes, and the astonishing choice of sushi, are as excellent as the views of the Bosphorus. Alfresco dining in the summer; chrome-and-white design all year. ⓐ Spor Caddesi, BJK Plaza A, Blok 48, Akaretler ① (0212) 227 4404 ⓦ www.istanbuldoors.com ① 12.00–02.00 (kitchen closes 24.00)

BARS & CLUBS

Blackk Located on the same waterfront street as Mado (see page 110), Blackk is an expensive and oh-so-trendy restaurant until 23.00... and then it transforms into a nightclub. The elegant tables become bar stands and the black décor gets blacker when the lights dim. ⓐ Muallim Naci Caddesi 71, Ortaköy ① (0212) 236 7256 ⓦ www. blackk.net ① 20.00–04.00 Tues–Sat (sometimes closes June–Sept)

Jazz Café Jazz and fusion lovers must try Jazz Café, where there are live performances all week, except Fridays and Saturdays. The building also serves food on both floors. ⓐ İstiklal Caddesi, Hasnun Galip 14 ⓣ (0212) 245 0516 ⓛ 20.00–04.00 Tues–Sat

Roxy Expect good gigs at this landmark venue on the Istanbul music scene, attracting a young crowd in their twenties. Famous for serving big bottles of 'Sex on the Beach' and consistently hosting worthy but varied music. ⓐ Sıraselviler Caddesi, Arslan Yatağı Sokak 7, Taksim ⓣ (0212) 249 1283 ⓦ www.roxy.com.tr ⓛ 21.00–05.00 Wed, Fri & Sat (closed June–Sept) ⓘ Admission charge

CINEMAS

AFM Fitaş Nearly a dozen screens for Turkish- and English-language films showing all the current releases. This multiplex is at the top end of İstiklal Caddesi, almost at Taksim Square, and there is an English-style pub and restaurant in the same building. ⓐ İstiklal Caddesi 24 ⓣ (0212) 251 2020 ⓦ www.afm.com.tr

Emek Cinema The street housing this historic cinema runs off İstiklal Caddesi. It is a real treat, a rococo-style picture palace with 875 seats and majestic décor, chosen (with good reason) to host the Istanbul Film Festival for the past two decades. ⓐ İstiklal Caddesi, Yeşilçam Sokak 5

ⓞ *Charming, colourful buildings line the Bosphorus*

OUT OF TOWN
trips

Exploring the Bosphorus

A trip along the Bosphorus completes any visit to Istanbul, and there are transport choices to suit your time and inclinations. The most popular route is the ferry from Eminönü that departs daily at 10.30, with extra services at midday in the summer, normally stopping at Beşiktaş, Kanlıca, Yeniköy, Sarıyer, Rumeli Kavağı and, usually the turnaround stop, Anadolu Kavağı. The trip one way takes nearly two hours and you cannot hop on and off along the way, so by the time you have returned you may feel you have seen too much of the Bosphorus and spent the whole day doing so. When the ferry reaches Anadolu Kavağı, instead of returning the same way, you could take a bus back to Üsküdar and then catch a ferry from there back to the European side.

Alternatives include disembarking before Anadolu Kavağı and returning to Istanbul by bus or taxi or, if you get off at Kanlıca, catching one of the regular ferries that ply their way back to Istanbul. The other alternative, taking about three hours in total, is to catch one of the smaller boats that depart from Eminönü and which usually travel only as far as Rumeli Kavağı, and stop there for a lunch break before making the return journey. A good-value trip of this kind is with **Tur Yol** (❶ (0212) 251 4421 Ⓦ www.turyol.com) – you will see their boats at Eminönü – who go as far as the second Bosphorus bridge, the Fatih Sultan Mehmet Bridge. Trips like these depart only when full, but that does not usually take too long in the summer.

A boat trip on the Bosphorus is not compulsory and you may wish to explore the area on land. Buses are frequent from Eminönü and Taksim Square and taxi rides are not inordinately expensive. The last bus back from Rumeli Kavağı to Eminönü is usually around 22.00, but if you wish to linger longer, you can catch a bus from

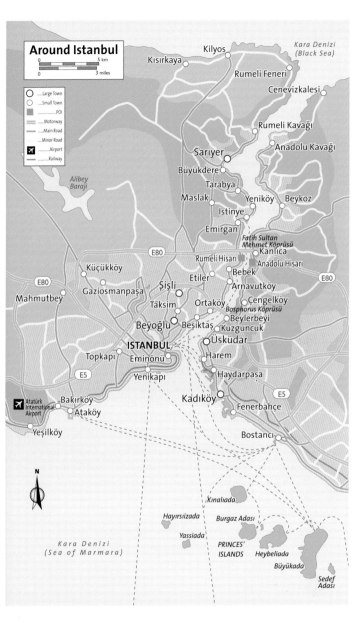

Rumeli Kavağı for the short hop to Sarıyer, and from there later buses run back to Taksim and Eminönü.

Cruise tours on the Bosphorus are run by the following:

International Travel Services (morning and afternoon cruises) ❶ (0212) 275 1870 Ⓦ www.dailycitytours.com

Senkron Travel Agency (afternoon cruises) ⓐ Arasta Bazaar 51, Sultanahmet ❶ (0212) 638 8340 Ⓦ www.senkrontours.com

SIGHTS & ATTRACTIONS

Arnavutköy

Arnavutköy, on the European side and halfway between the Bosphorus and the Fatih bridges, retains more of its waterside village charms than most locations this close to the shore. The grand wooden houses, *yalıs*, by the waterfront are attractive, and away from the shoreline there are more picturesque homes built from wood.
Ⓝ Bus: 40T

Bebek & Hidiv Kasrı (Khedive's Palace)

Bebek, where some of the seriously rich have their second homes, is a 15-minute stroll from Arnavutköy along a promenade and, amid all the restaurants, shoreline cafés and speciality shops, is Hidiv Kasrı (Khedive's Palace), now the Egyptian Consulate. A lovely Art Nouveau building built by the last khedive of Egypt, it is situated by the ferry stop. Cevdet Paşa Caddesi is the Bosphorus-facing main street and there is an attractive park suitable for picnicking.

Kuzguncuk

On the Asian shoreline and easy to reach by bus from Üsküdar or a ferry from Beşiktaş, Kuzguncuk is a low-key village with a good

▲ *The Asian side of the Bosphorus*

◠ The magnificent suspension bridge beside the Ortaköy Mosque

BOSPHORUS BRIDGE

This was the first bridge to be built across the Bosphorus, if you don't include the pontoon bridges erected by the Persians when they attempted to conquer the ancient Greeks. It was finished on 29 August 1973 to mark the 50th anniversary of the inauguration of the Turkish Republic. A graceful structure and ranked as the sixth longest in the suspension bridge world league, it measures 1,560 m (5,120 ft) in length. If you were 64 m (210 ft) tall, you could touch it when standing on the water below. You can't walk across it; just enjoy the view.

ⓝ Bus: 40T from Taksim Square to Ortaköy

restaurant (İsmet Baba, see page 128) and an interesting Jewish cemetery where the tombstones lie flat on the ground. The cemetery dates back to the 15th century, when Jews fleeing the Spanish Inquisition were given asylum in Istanbul. You can walk to the cemetery via İcadiye Sokak. ⓝ Bus: 15 or 15P from Üsküdar

Rumeli Hisarı (Fortress of Europe)

A fortress built by Mehmet the Conqueror in 1452 in four months, at a narrow point on the Bosphorus, as an opening move in the conquest of Constantinople. Facing it across the straits is Anadolu Hisarı, the Fortress of Asia, and between them a vital supply line to the city was cut off. Later a prison, the Rumeli Hisarı is now used in the summer as a venue for the International Istanbul Music Festival. You can walk here along the promenade from Bebek in 15 minutes. ⓐ Yahya Kemal Caddesi ⓣ (0212) 263 5305 ⓛ 09.00–16.30 Thur–Tues ⓘ Admission charge

Rumeli Kavağı & Anadolu Kavağı

Rumeli Kavağı is the last ferry stop on the European side and a pleasant place to enjoy lunch at one of the many fish restaurants clustered around the jetty. Just as attractive for a meal is Anadolu Kavağı, almost directly opposite on the Asian side, and the place where you are more likely to have lunch if arriving on the main ferry from Eminönü because there is a stopover here for a couple of hours before the ferry sets off on the return journey. All the restaurants buy their fish locally so it'll be as fresh as it can be. There should also be time, especially if you have brought a picnic lunch, to walk up to the remains of a Byzantine fortress on the hill overlooking the village.

CULTURE

Küçüksu Kasrı (Küçüksu Palace)

Küçüksu Palace, on the Asian side, is another building superbly placed for maximum effect when approached from the water. The interior is filled with plush trimmings and accoutrements fit for a sultan, as was the intention when the building was completed in the 1850s. The visual highlight is the grand double staircase that curves up to the entrance. ⓐ Küçüksu Caddesi, Çengelköy ⓣ (0216) 323 3303 ⓛ 09.00–17.00 Tues, Wed & Fri–Sun (until 16.00 in winter) ⓥ Bus: 15 or 15P from Üsküdar to Çengelköy ⓘ Admission charge

Sadberk Hanım Müzesi (Sadberk Hanım Museum)

This museum incorporates two classically styled *yalıs* (wooden summer villas) for its displays of ethnographic and archaeological artefacts. An engaging and eclectic collection that includes Assyrian cuneiform tablets, ancient Greek pottery, a circumcision bed and extraordinarily fine Turkish embroideries. ⓐ Piyasa Caddesi 27, Büyükdere, Sarıyer

◭ *Anadolu Kavağı*

Pablo Picasso (1881-1973), Büst / Kadın 07.07.1971, © Succession Picasso 2005

World-class exhibitions are held at the Sakıp Sabancı Museum

🕿 (0212) 242 3813 🌐 www.sadberkhanimmuzesi.org.tr 🕑 10.00–17.00 Thur–Tues 🚢 Ferry: Sarıyer; bus: 25T

Sakıp Sabancı Müzesi (Sakıp Sabancı Museum)

This art gallery stunned Turkey in 2006 by bringing to the country the most important exhibition it has ever known, in the form of 135 works by Picasso. Quite unsurprisingly, Turkish people travelled here from every corner of the land to see works they never dreamt would be exhibited on home soil. Such an exhibition does not seem just to have been a flash in the cultural pan, so be sure to check out what is on and consider coming here anyway for the superb gallery restaurant, Müzedechanga (see page 128). 🏛 Sakıp Sabancı Caddesi 42, Emirgan 🕿 (0212) 277 2200 🌐 http://muze.sabanciuniv.edu 🕑 10.00–18.00 Tues, Thur, Fri & Sun, 10.00–22.00 Wed 🛈 Admission charge

RETAIL THERAPY

Bebek Badem Ezmecisi A purchase worth considering in this specialist sweet shop is the almond marzipan, but your sweet tooth may also be seduced by the glass jars of sweets that fill the shelves. 🏛 Cevdet Paşa Caddesi 53C, Bebek 🕿 (0212) 263 5984 🕑 09.00–22.30

Laleli Zeytinyağları Like Bebek Badem Ezmecisi, this is a family-run shop but this time selling its own olive oils. There is quite a variety and some olive-based bathroom products are also available. 🏛 Cevdet Paşa Caddesi 46D, Bebek 🕿 (0212) 265 6617 🌐 www.zeytinim.com 🕑 10.00–19.00 Mon–Sat, 11.00–16.00 Sun

Sedef Gür Butik One-off designs and specialist clothing and accessories. 🏛 Les Ottomans Hotel, Muallim Naci Caddesi 68,

just before Bebek on the Bosphorus Way ☎ (0212) 359 1500
🕐 09.00–22.00

TAKING A BREAK

Asırlık Kanlıca Yoğurdu £ Kanlıca, on the Asian side, is famous for its yoghurt. This is not the only place where it can be enjoyed, but it is easy to find and convenient, being situated next to the ferry terminal. @ İskele Square, Kanlıca ☎ (0216) 413 4469 🕐 09.00–24.00

Bebek Kahvesi £ A pleasantly unpretentious café that draws in locals throughout the day and evening for a chat and game of backgammon. Tasty apple pie made daily. @ Cevdet Paşa Caddesi 18A, Bebek ☎ (0212) 257 5402 🕐 06.00–23.00 (summer); 06.00–21.00 (winter)

Zeynel £ A deservedly famous ice-cream parlour, in the same family since the 1920s, with over a dozen varieties to choose from – including some that, apparently, won't damage your waistline – and some delicious desserts. @ Köybaşı Caddesi 136, Yeniköy ☎ (0212) 262 8987 🕐 06.30–24.00 Mon–Sat, 08.00–24.00 Sun

Ali Baba Köftecisi £–££ Arnavutköy boasts a number of fish restaurants that could be checked out for a night-time visit. During the day, though, it is hard to beat Ali Baba Köftecisi (there are two outlets in the same street) for a lunch of meatballs and *piyaz* (beans cooked in olive oil) followed by one of the simple desserts. @ 1 Cadde 69, Arnavutköy ☎ (0212) 265 3612 🕐 12.00–21.30

Bebek Brasserie & Pastry Shop £–££ If picnicking in Bebek Park, pick up some pastries here, or tuck into one of their sushi meals. At weekends their breakfast buffet is a big draw. ⓐ Cevdet Paşa Caddesi 28A, Bebek ❶ (0212) 257 7270 ⓛ Pastry shop: 08.30–21.00; restaurant: 09.00–20.00

Lucca ££–£££ A café that changes its mood as the day progresses, becoming noisy with loud music at night. During the day it is a good place for a drink or snack. ⓐ Cevdet Paşa Caddesi 51, Bebek ❶ (0212) 257 1255 ⓛ 10.00–02.00

⬤ Take a break and enjoy a refreshing Turkish tea

AFTER DARK

RESTAURANTS

Sade Kahve £–££ Turkish, bohemian-style café-restaurant on the waterfront and with the Fatih Bridge in view. The café is downstairs but climb the stairs for the marble-floored restaurant and outdoor tables. ❷ Yahya Kemal Caddesi 20A, Rumeli Hisarı ☏ (0212) 358 2324 🌐 www.sadekahve.com 🕐 07.00–02.00 (summer); 07.00–24.00 (winter)

Müzedechanga ££–£££ Views of the Bosphorus wherever you sit in this glass-fronted restaurant at the Sakıp Sabancı Museum, and crafted Turkish delights like *karanfilli köfte* (carnation Turkish meatballs), *zeytinyağlı kereviz* (olive-oil-based celery roots) and *pişmaniye* (Turkish-style candyfloss). ❸ Sakıp Sabancı Caddesi 42, Emirgan ☏ (0212) 323 0901 🌐 www.changa-istanbul.com 🕐 10.30–01.00 Tues–Sun

Yakamoz ££–£££ A seafront restaurant with a panoramic view of the Bosphorus on the seafront. The speciality is fresh fish, but you should also come at the weekend for a slap-up breakfast. ❸ İskele Meydanı 1, Kanlıca, near the pier ☏ (0212) 527 6859 🌐 www.yakamozbalik.com 🕐 08.00–24.00

İskele £££ A seafood restaurant plonked on a restored old pier near the Rumeli Hisarı fortress. ❸ Yahya Kemal Caddesi 1, Rumeli Hisarı ☏ (0212) 263 2997 🌐 www.rumelihisariiskele.com 🕐 12.00–24.00

İsmet Baba £££ A great, waterfront fish restaurant where the mezes (Turkish starters) are a feast and the fish is always fresh. ❸ İcadiye Caddesi 96, Kuzguncuk ☏ (0216) 553 1232 🌐 www.ismetbaba.com.tr 🕐 12.00–00.30 (kitchen closes 22.30)

Lacivert £££ This place is under the Fatih Sultan Mehmet Bridge and the restaurant boat will pick up diners from the European side. Mediterranean cuisine with a Turkish accent, and an above-average wine list. ❷ Körfez Caddesi 57A, Anadolu Hisarı ❶ (0216) 413 4224 ❿ www.lacivertrestaurant.com ⏱ 12.00–23.00 Mon–Sat, 11.00–14.00 Sun (buffet breakfast)

Poseidon £££ As the name and location would suggest, this is a seafood restaurant and the most glamorous place for dining and wining in Bebek. ❷ Cevdet Paşa Caddesi 58, Bebek ❶ (0212) 263 3823 ❿ www.poseidonbebek.com ⏱ 12.00–01.00

ACCOMMODATION

Bebek £££ A plush and expensive hotel where the best rooms have their own balconies overlooking the Bosphorus (viewless rooms benefit from a hefty discount). ❷ Cevdet Paşa Caddesi 34, Bebek ❶ (0212) 358 2000 ❿ www.bebekhotel.com.tr

Bosphorus Palace £££ A Special-status hotel on the Asian side, a tastefully renovated *yalı* (wooden summer villa) with large rooms and a rather posh restaurant. ❷ Yalıboyu Caddesi 64, Beylerbeyi ❶ (0216) 422 0003 ❿ www.bosphoruspalace.com

Sumahan £££ A luxury boutique hotel on the Asian shoreline, with its own slice of waterfront, six rooms, twelve suites and a private launch service across the Bosphorus. The hotel also has two restaurants, a wellness centre with *hamam* and massage facilities, and 24-hour room service. A place to spoil yourself. ❷ Kuleli Caddesi 51, Çengelköy ❶ (0216) 422 8000 ❿ www.sumahan.com

Into Asia

It is easy to hop across the Bosphorus on one of the many daily ferries that depart from Eminönü or Karaköy and, if Üsküdar is your destination instead of Karaköy, there are also ferries from Beşiktaş. A suggested itinerary for a full day's excursion is to catch a morning ferry to Kadıköy and walk up to Bahariye Caddesi to explore the shops, cafés and restaurants. After lunch, walk back to Rıhtım Caddesi, the road facing the sea, and take a *dolmuş* (mini-van) for a ten-minute journey to Üsküdar. The *dolmuş* stop for the mini-vans to Üsküdar is clearly marked on Rıhtım Caddesi. After exploring Üsküdar, take a ferry back from there to the European side. Ferrying out to the Princes' Islands can be a full-day excursion in itself. Please note – when travelling on the ferry to Kadıköy, do not disembark at the first stop – this is Haydarpaşa Railway Station – but the second and main stop at the Kadıköy terminal.

SIGHTS & ATTRACTIONS

Bahariye Caddesi

This is the street in Kadıköy to head for after disembarking from the ferry. Turn right after exiting the ferry terminal and walk along to the main junction, then cross the road and head uphill on Söğütlü Çeşme Caddesi, which begins next to the big, blue-glassed Türkiye İş Bankası. Continue up this street until you reach the junction with the sculptured metal bull in the middle and turn to the right for Bahariye Caddesi. Filled with a range of shops and places to eat, the side streets running off on either side of Bahariye Caddesi are the ones to explore for funky little cafés, bars and restaurants.

İskele Camii (Dock Mosque)

Facing you at the Üsküdar ferry port is a large building known variously as İskele Mosque, Mihrimah Sultan Mosque and Dock Mosque. This Ottoman-style mosque was built in the mid 16th century for the daughter of Süleyman the Magnificent by Mimar Sinan (see page 81). Today it offers good views of the Üsküdar port

⏏ *Architecture on Büyükada befitting a Prince's Island*

PRINCES' ISLANDS

Nine islands in the Sea of Marmara make up the Princes' Islands. There are no cars – only horse-drawn carriages – so the islands make a peaceful break from the city traffic. Heybeliada is perhaps the prettiest island, while Büyükada is the largest and most cosmopolitan with plenty of hotels, restaurants, cafés and a nice sandy beach, Eskibağ at Haliki Bay. Small boats will transport you from the pier to the beach for free. The St George Monastery, or Aya Yorgi (Hagia Yorgi) Church, dating back to Byzantine times, is situated at Yücetepe, which is the highest point on Büyükada. On 23 April and 24 September, tens of thousands of visitors of every faith walk the steep path up to the monastery as a form of pilgrimage. You can also take a horse-drawn tour of the island before walking up to Aya Yorgi.

Ferries depart from the docks at Kabataş or Kadıköy and stop at the four largest islands: Kınalıada, Burgaz Adası, Heybeliada and finally Büyükada. Some ferries also go to Büyükada directly from Bostancı in 30 minutes.

scene from its elegant colonnaded exterior. ⓐ Hakimiyeti Milliye Caddesi, Üsküdar ⓛ 08.00–18.00

Kız Kulesi (Maiden's Tower)

Offshore from Üsküdar, the tower on the islet is called Maiden's Tower after the legend of an incarcerated princess who died here. It is also called Leander's Tower, pirating the Greek legend of the hero Leander who swam a strait between Europe and Asia (not here

◆ *The Maiden's Tower, on the Bosphorus*

but in the Dardanelles hundreds of miles away) to meet his lover Hero in a tower. Film buffs may recall the islet's use as a location in the James Bond film *The World Is Not Enough*. The tower can be visited by small boats departing from a nearby pier, and it's also a sight to be seen clearly from the shoreline or from on board the ferry. Ⓦ www.kizkulesi.com.tr

CULTURE

Atik Valide Camii (Atik Valide Mosque)

The hillside location is too far away to reach on foot from Üsküdar ferry terminal and a taxi is the best way to get to this large and aesthetically very satisfying mosque complex, designed by the hugely talented Sinan (see page 81). The richly decorated interior of the Atik Valide Camii is worthy of your time. One apse is beautifully covered in *İznik* tiles, the galleries boast *trompe-l'œil* paintings and the window shutters are inlaid with mother-of-pearl and ivory.
ⓐ Çinili Camii Sokak, Üsküdar Ⓛ 08.00–18.00

Selimiye Barracks & Florence Nightingale Museum

The main reason for arranging a trip to these barracks, used as a military hospital during the Crimean War (1853–6), is to visit the Florence Nightingale Museum. The part of the barracks where the 'Lady of the Lamp' worked constitutes the museum and visits have to be arranged in advance by faxing a request; the fax should include the photograph page of your passport, the intended time of your visit (giving 24 hours' notice), and the contact telephone number of your hotel (state the room number) so that your visit time can be confirmed. ⓐ Çeşme-i Kebir Caddesi, Selimiye, Üsküdar
Ⓣ (0216) 556 8000/553 1009 Ⓕ (0216) 310 7929 Ⓛ 09.00–17.00

● *Performing pre-prayer ablutions at the Yeni Valide Camii in Üsküdar*

Yeni Valide Camii (Yeni Valide Mosque)

This second of the two mosques close to Üsküdar ferry terminal is entered through a large gateway and across a courtyard area. It was built in the early 18th century by a sultan in honour of his mother.
⊘ Demokrasi Meydanı, Hakimiyeti Milliye Caddesi, Üsküdar
● 08.00–18.00

RETAIL THERAPY

Artemis Hediyelik The perfect gift shop, with more than 5,000 handicrafts from all over Africa and Asia. Also check out the beautiful wooden furniture and statues. ⊘ Yoğurtçu Sütcü Sokak 48, Kadıköy
❶ (0216) 349 2750 ● 08.30–20.30 Mon–Sat

İnci The famous İnci shoe shop was established in 1917 as a modest shoeshine parlour – it's not cheap, but it's worth it. ⓐ Bahariye Caddesi 23, Kadıköy ⓣ (0216) 347 6120 ⓦ www.incideri.com.tr ⓛ 09.00–21.00 Mon–Sat, 12.00–20.00 Sun

Kervan Opposite the ferry in Üsküdar, this shop retails cushion covers, gorgeous embroidered quilt covers and a variety of home furnishings, some of which will fit into that extra piece of luggage you bought to carry home your booty. ⓐ Selmanağa Caddesi 89, Üsküdar ⓣ (0216) 343 9530 ⓦ www.krvn.com.tr ⓛ 09.30–20.00 Mon–Fri, 12.00–20.00 Sat & Sun

TAKING A BREAK

İsis Café £ Sit out in the garden, warm up by the attic fireplace with a glass of hot wine or find a spot on one of three nicely decorated floors, depending on your mood. Choose from a variety of pastas, salads and meat dishes. ⓐ Kadife Sokak 26, Kadıköy, near the Greek Orthodox Church ⓣ (0216) 349 7381 ⓦ www.isisrest.com ⓛ 11.00–01.30

Mozaik Café £ Seek out this little café for a pleasant light lunch away from the Kadıköy hubbub. Walk up Bahariye Caddesi and turn right into Sakızgülü Sokak. Miralay Nazım Sokak is the first turning on the right and the café is halfway down on the left side. The menu is not in English but you will not find it too difficult to work out, consisting as it does of pasta, crêpes, pizza, sandwiches and salads. ⓐ Miralay Nazım Sokak 30/2, off Sakızgülü Sokak, off Bahariye Caddesi, Kadıköy ⓣ (0216) 337 4920 ⓛ 09.00–23.00

⬥ *Cosy atmosphere in an old Turkish café*

Murat £ On the corner of Rıhtım Caddesi where the sign to the My Dora hotel hangs, roughly opposite the ferry terminal, glass-fronted Murat has a huge menu in Turkish but it is best to just see what is on display at the counter and pick what takes your fancy. This restaurant is very popular and fresh dishes are cooked daily.
🅐 Rıhtım Caddesi, Kadıköy 🕾 (0216) 338 3737 🕒 05.00–01.00

Arka Oda £–££ A place to listen to great music, with an interesting programme of performers from around the world. 🅐 Kadife Sokak 18A, Kadıköy 🕾 (0216) 418 0277 🕸 www.arkaoda.com 🕒 13.00–02.00

Yücetepe Café £–££ On the grounds of St George Monastery on Büyükada (see page 132), this café serves good salads, grilled meat and sausage sandwiches. Wine comes from Bozcaada, another of the Princes' Islands. ⓐ Yücetepe Mevki, Büyükada, near the Aya Yorgi Church ⓣ (0216) 382 1333 ⓦ www.yucetepe.com ⓛ 10.00–24.00 daily (summer); 10.00–18.00 Sat & Sun (winter)

AFTER DARK

Kadıköy is the best area for nightlife. The small streets off Bahariye Caddesi are full of café-bars and restaurants. You could also explore Kadife Sokak, known as Barlar Sokağı (meaning 'Street of Bars'), for music and cultural performances. Although smaller than Beyoğlu, it's cosmopolitan, young and trendy. Just give yourself time to get downhill for the last ferry back at 23.00 (check the time when you arrive).

RESTAURANTS

Mix £–££ Easy to find, commanding a prime site by the junction with the metal-sculpted bull where Bahariye Caddesi begins, Mix is a café-restaurant during the day but at night the fairy lights are switched on and live music enlivens the atmosphere. There is a courtyard with tables if the music is too loud. Choose from a menu of Turkish dishes, pizza, salads and burgers.
ⓐ Bahariye Caddesi, Nihal Sokak 13, Kadıköy ⓣ (0216) 349 8750
ⓛ 08.00–24.00

Mavi ££–£££ One of the best fish restaurants in the Princes' Islands, this restaurant is known for its delicious platters with prawn pastries and flavoursome Aegean herbs. ⓐ Yalı Caddesi 29, Heybeliada, opposite the IDO port ⓣ (0216) 351 0128 ⓦ www.mavirestaurant.net
ⓛ 08.00–24.00

Sözbir Royal Residence £££ A hotel in Üsküdar across from the ferry terminal, where you can enjoy drinks in the lobby café while gazing out across the Bosphorus or have lunch in the rather posh restaurant that also faces the sea. ❷ Paşalimanı Caddesi 6, Üsküdar ❶ (0216) 495 7000 Ⓦ www.sozbirhotel.com ❺ 07.30–24.00

CINEMA

Rexx Sineması One of the oldest cinemas in Kadıköy – in the 1900s, the building housed the famous Apollon Theater. Current Hollywood films normally feature on the weekly programme. ❷ Bahariye Caddesi, Sakızgülü Sokak 20–22, Kadıköy ❶ (0216) 336 0112 Ⓦ www.rexx-online.com

ACCOMMODATION

Hush Hostel £–££ A renovated Ottoman villa in Kadıköy, often hosting art exhibitions on the ground floor. ❷ Miralay Nazım Sokak 20, Kadıköy ❶ (0216) 330 9188 Ⓦ www.hushhostelistanbul.com

Aden ££ Tucked away down an alley off the main Rıhtım Caddesi, it is almost directly opposite the ferry station. Functional but smart, fine for a one-night stay and with its own restaurant. ❷ Rıhtım Caddesi, Yoğurtçu Şükrü Sokak 2, Kadıköy ❶ (0216) 345 1000 Ⓦ www.adenotel.com

Bella ££ Next to the Aden but in a higher league, this is a new hotel where comfort and simplicity are modishly aligned. There is no restaurant, though breakfast is included in room rates, but you'll find a *hamam* and sauna downstairs. ❷ Rıhtım Caddesi, Yoğurtçu Şükrü Sokak 5, Kadıköy ❶ (0216) 349 7373

My Dora ££ In a similar price bracket to Bella, My Dora (signposted on Rıhtım Caddesi) has an interesting Modernist polished steel-and-glass lobby. Bedrooms are fairly small and slightly old-fashioned in terms of décor, but they do have minibars and modern bathrooms. There is a restaurant on the first floor. ⊖ Rıhtım Caddesi, Recaizade Sokak 6, Kadıköy ☎ (0216) 414 8350 ⓦ www.hotelmydora.com

Büyükada Princess £££ If you take a trip to Princes' Island and want to sleep in style without bothering about your budget, this attractive stone-built hotel is the place to come. There's a pool and restaurant too. ⊖ 23 Nisan Caddesi 2, Büyükada ☎ (0216) 382 1628 ⓦ www.buyukadaprincess.com

Sözbir Royal Residence £££ Turn to the left after exiting from the ferry terminal to find this hotel on the other side of the road after a three-minute walk. Very plush indeed, the hotel boasts Ottoman-style luxury, with rooms and an outdoor pool facing the Bosphorus. ⊖ Paşalimanı Caddesi 6, Üsküdar ☎ (0216) 495 7000 ⓦ www.sozbirhotel.com

Splendid £££ A hotel that earns its name because of its location on a hill and the simple elegance of the wooden building. It offers an outdoor pool, rooms with balconies and a restaurant. The rooms are not quite as splendid but are fine for a one-night stay. ⊖ 23 Nisan Caddesi 53, Büyükada ☎ (0216) 382 6950 ⓦ www.splendidhotel.net ❶ Closed Nov–Apr

---

● *Sirkeci Railway Station was the original terminus for the Orient Express*

PRACTICAL
information

Directory

GETTING THERE
By air
Turkish Airlines (Ⓦ www.turkishairlines.com), **British Airways**
(Ⓦ www.britishairways.com) and **easyJet** (Ⓦ www.easyjet.com) all
fly direct from the UK to Istanbul in around three and a half hours.
Turkish Airlines and British Airways flights go from London Heathrow
to Atatürk International Airport (see page 48), on the European side,
while easyJet flies from Gatwick and Luton to the smaller Sabiha
Gökçen Airport on the Asian side (see page 48). **Delta Airlines**
(Ⓦ www.delta.com) flies direct from New York and San Francisco in
the US, and Turkish Airlines has flights from Chicago and New York.
Most major European airlines have direct flights from European
capitals to Istanbul.

A number of companies offer package deals to Istanbul that
include flights and accommodation, which can be good value. There
are many companies, but you can start by trying **Anatolian Sky
Holidays** (ⓘ +44 121 764 3550 Ⓦ www.anatoliansky.co.uk) and **Cachet
Travel** (ⓘ +44 20 8847 8700 Ⓦ www.cachet-travel.co.uk).

Many people are aware that air travel emits CO_2, which contributes
to climate change. You may be interested in the possibility of lessening
the environmental impact of your flight through the charity **Climate
Care** (Ⓦ www.climatecare.org), which offsets your CO_2 by funding
environmental projects around the world.

By rail
No, it is not possible to take the Orient Express to Istanbul but, if you
have a lot of time and love trains, you can spend three nights and
four days getting there from London via Brussels, Vienna and

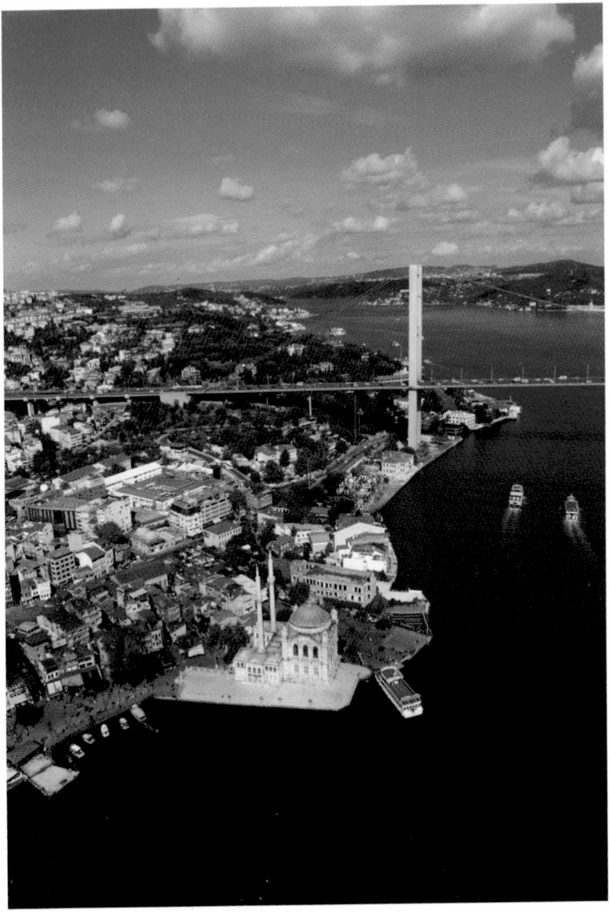

An aerial view over the city

Budapest. It will take less time from cities on the European continent but the cost is still likely to exceed an air fare. European travellers will save some money with an Inter-Rail pass. Some good sites to check out for information are:

The Man in Seat Sixty-One Ⓦ www.seat61.com

Rail Europe Ⓦ www.raileurope.co.uk (UK), www.eurorailways.com (US)

Thomas Cook European Rail Timetable ☎ +44 1733 416477 (UK)
Ⓦ www.thomascookpublishing.com

By road

Unless you want to drive through Hungary, Romania and Bulgaria, the more familiar road route is through France, Italy and Greece, with the option of a direct ferry from Italy to the west coast of Turkey and then a drive to Istanbul. Registration documents and driving licences need to be brought with you. Check with your insurance company regarding insurance cover.

ENTRY FORMALITIES

All visitors to Turkey require a current passport with at least three months' validity remaining. Some nationalities, including citizens of the UK, Ireland and the US, also require a visa. The standard tourist visa lasts for three months. It is issued at your point of entry into the country and is not available in advance from a Turkish embassy or consulate. Note that it must be paid for in cash in your home currency, so make sure you have enough with you. For citizens of the UK, the cost is currently £10; for Ireland €15; for the US $20. These are subject to change, however, so see Ⓦ www.mfa.gov.tr (click 'Consular Info') for up-to-date prices before departing. Citizens of Denmark, France, Germany, Greece, New Zealand (and some other non-EU countries) do not require a visa. Costs vary for other nationalities.

Import limits for EU and non-EU travellers include two litres of spirits or wine and 1,000 cigarettes. There are strict rules on the export of antiquities, including antique carpets, and any reputable antique dealer should be able to advise you on this and arrange for the necessary paperwork.

MONEY

The new Turkish lira (YTL) replaced the old Turkish lira (TL) in 2005, making the older notes obsolete and dropping six zeros from the value of the lira. On 1 January 2009 the word 'new' (*yeni*) was removed and the Turkish lira regained its former name, TL. Since January 2010, new Turkish lira (YTL) bills and coins are no longer in circulation. TL notes are in denominations of 5, 10, 20, 50, 100 and 200. One Turkish lira is divided into 100 kurus (Kr), with coins in denominations of 1, 5, 10, 25 and 50 kurus and a 1 lira coin.

Currency can be exchanged in banks and exchange offices but the easiest way to obtain Turkish money is by using ATM machines. These are found outside banks among other useful locations and are easy to locate. However, it makes sense to bring a spare debit or credit card, some cash in your home currency or some traveller's cheques as a backup in case your wallet is lost or stolen.

Credit cards are readily accepted in many hotels, shops and restaurants but you may have to pay an extra commission. It is generally easiest to pay in cash if possible, especially in shops and restaurants.

The changes to the lira over the past few years have created a mini-spate of unscrupulous types trying to offload redundant currency on unsuspecting tourists. Do not accept the old Turkish lira notes, easy to spot as they are all numbered in millions – 1,000,000, 5,000,000, 10,000,000, and so on. Also reject new Turkish lira (YTL) notes. Beware of poor-grade counterfeit notes being passed on by the drivers of lone taxis you pick up on the road or at transport hubs (it's generally safer to pick up taxis from designated ranks). If in doubt, jot down the licence plate of the car to be able to report it later on.

HEALTH, SAFETY & CRIME

There are no compulsory vaccinations but your doctor may advise inoculation against hepatitis A and B, tetanus and typhoid.

Tap water is chlorinated and safe for brushing teeth but for drinking it is best to use the bottled water that is available everywhere in the city. Should you suffer from a mild stomach complaint or diarrhoea, pharmacies (*eczane*) sell standard treatments and oral rehydration salts. Pharmacies have English-speaking staff and should be consulted for minor complaints. If you require more attention and prescription drugs, there are many excellent public and private clinics (*poliklinik*) in Istanbul. Private hospitals are preferable to state hospitals. See the 'Emergencies' section (page 154) for contact details.

Istanbul is as safe as any other major European city and common sense dictates precautions as regards personal possessions and safety. Pickpockets operate in crowded places like the bazaars and İstiklal Caddesi. Have a list of your traveller's cheque numbers and keep this with your proof of purchase (which will be needed for a claim) and the contact number to use in case the cheques are lost or stolen. Keep this information separate from the cheques themselves; sending them to an email account is a good idea. Keep a photocopy of the main page of your passport and the page with the stamp of your Turkish visa and keep these separate from your passport. Consider keeping the number of your passport, or a scanned copy of the relevant pages, in an email which can be retrieved if necessary.

See page 154 for emergency contact telephone numbers. Some useful websites are:

American travel advice Ⓦ www.cdc.gov/travel and www.health finder.com

British government health and travel advice Ⓦ www.dh.gov.uk and www.fco.gov.uk/travel

Travel Health UK online Ⓦ www.travelhealth.co.uk

Useful tips and information Ⓦ www.tripprep.com

World Health Organization Ⓦ www.who.int

It is advisable to arrange travel insurance before travelling to Istanbul as there are no reciprocal health schemes with EU countries. A good policy will cover medical treatment, baggage, and theft or loss of possessions. You will need to make a police report for non-medical claims and ensure you keep any receipts for medical treatment. Consider keeping a copy of your policy and emergency contact numbers in your email account.

OPENING HOURS

Opening hours of museums and attractions are usually from 08.30 or 09.00 to 17.30 or 18.00 and some smaller places close for a lunch hour. Government office hours are 08.00 to noon and 13.30 to 17.00, Monday to Saturday. Banks have similar hours but open at 08.30. General shopping hours are 09.00 to 17.00 Monday to Saturday, but many stay open until 19.00 or 20.00. Markets are open from around 08.30 to around 19.00.

TOILETS

Public toilets are easy to find in Istanbul, marked *Erkekler* for men and *Bayanlar* for women, but are mostly of the squat type and are not always kept clean. An attendant is usually around to collect a small charge and may supply toilet paper but don't rely on this;

carry your own anyway. Many travellers prefer to make use of hotels' flush toilets and the facilities in any good restaurant they visit.

CHILDREN

There are not that many sites or attractions that are obviously suited to children and hours spent in mosques and museums are likely to bore them. One exception is the Archaeological Museum (see page 63), which has a special children's section, including a hands-on model of the Trojan Horse and a medieval castle for clambering about in. The underground Basilica Cistern (see page 63) is also capable of engaging children's interest.

On the plus side, children are adored by Turkish people and there will be few problems accommodating them in restaurants and hotels. Children under 6 usually stay for free in hotels, with a 50 per cent discount for those aged between 6 and 15. Some of the better hotels will provide cots and arrange baby-sitting through an agency. Baby foods and disposable nappies are available in supermarkets and pharmacies.

By way of excursions, a boat trip up the Bosphorus (see page 116) should appeal to children but in the summer be sure to arrive well before departure time to secure seats with a view. It takes nearly two hours to reach Anadolu Kavağı, the turnabout point on the boat trip, but if this is too long for your children you could always disembark at Kanlıca and then take a taxi across the Fatih Bridge to visit Rumeli Hisarı (see page 121). The ramparts and towers of this fortress can be explored by children but there are few safety features so take extra care and don't let them explore unaccompanied. Alternatively, take the 15A bus back from the turnabout point to Kanlıca and then a taxi to Rumeli Hisarı.

Young children should also enjoy a trip to the car-free Princes' Islands (see page 132) where bicycles can be hired – but be sure to choose a well-maintained bike. There are donkey rides in Büyükada in summer.

🔵 *Take a taxi across the Fatih Bridge to Rumeli Hisarı*

COMMUNICATIONS

Internet

Internet access is readily available throughout the city, either in Internet cafés or in your hotel. The municipality provides free Wi-Fi access in İstiklal Caddesi. Some restaurants and cafés also provide free Wi-Fi connections for their customers.

Phone

Public phones are everywhere and international calls can be made from most of them. Most calls are still made using phonecards, though an increasing number of payphones also accept credit cards. The new multimedia payphones also have facilities for SMS, MMS, email, video calls and Internet access. Phonecards are either prepaid cards in denominations of 50, 100, 200 and 350 units, or credit-card-sized TT cards with a scratch strip on the back and a 12-digit number to dial before making your call. Both types can be purchased from booths near clusters of telephones or from post offices.

As is usually the case with hotels, telephone rates for calls made from your bedroom have a significant mark-up. Mobile reception is good throughout the city and you should be able to make and receive calls and text on your mobile phone. Check with your home network before departure regarding the cost of calls and text messages abroad, as they may be higher than you expect.

Directory enquiries ⓘ 11811

International operator ⓘ 0800 314 0115

Post

The letters PTT (Post, Telephone and Telecommunications) identify post offices, usually open 09.00–1700 Monday to Saturday. The city's **Central Post Office** (ⓐ Şehinşah Pehlevi Caddesi) in Eminönü has a

TELEPHONING TURKEY

To telephone Turkey from abroad, dial first 00, then the country code for Turkey (90), then the area code (e.g. 212 for European Istanbul, 216 for Asian Istanbul), followed by the local seven-digit number. For local calls in Istanbul just dial the seven-digit number unless you are making a call to the Asian side from the European side, in which case dial 0216 followed by the number. To call the European side from the Asian side, dial 0212.

TELEPHONING FROM TURKEY

To make an international call from Turkey, dial 00, the international access code, then the country code, followed by the local area code minus the initial 0, and then the number.

Country codes: Australia 61; Canada 1; New Zealand 64; Republic of Ireland 353; South Africa 27; UK 44; US 1

24-hour section for making calls, sending and receiving faxes and buying stamps, and the branches at Atatürk Airport, Beyoğlu and Sirkeci are also open 24 hours (but with limited services at night). Stamps are available from post offices and PTT kiosks. Post boxes are yellow in colour and labelled PTT and many have slots marked *yurtdışı* (international), *şehiriçi* (local) for Istanbul and *yurtiçi* (domestic) for non-Istanbul, Turkish mail. A standard letter or postcard sent to anywhere in Turkey costs 0.75TL at the time of writing. International rates are 1.00TL for a standard letter and 0.90TL for a postcard. You can find a full listing of prices for parcels and heavier letters on the official PTT website ⓦ www.ptt.gov.tr

ELECTRICITY

The electricity rate is the normal European one of 220 V, 50 Hz, which means European appliances will work without a problem. Plugs come in the form of two round prongs so you may need an adaptor. American appliances using 110 V to 120 V will need an adaptor and a transformer. Mid-range and more expensive hotels will have 110-V shaver outlets. See Ⓦ www.kropla.com for more information. But the electricity infrastructure of some central places like Taksim is rather old, so you should take care to protect sensitive equipment like computers against voltage fluctuations, with personal surge protectors and the like.

TRAVELLERS WITH DISABILITIES

Istanbul is not yet fully geared up to receive travellers with disabilities. Most museums and other places of interest, including mosques, are not well equipped for wheelchair users and other visitors with limited mobility or sight. Streets and pavements can be cracked and uneven and rarely have sloping kerbs. Accessible toilets are also uncommon and public transport can present a challenge. It is advisable to travel with a companion who can help where necessary.

When booking a hotel, try to talk to an English-speaking manager in order to establish that it has the facilities you require, and do be clear and specific about your needs in writing as well as over the phone. Ideally, find someone in Istanbul who can go there in person and make an assessment or send you some photos of the facilities.

The **Association of Turkish Travel Agents** (Ⓣ (0212) 259 8404 Ⓦ www.tursab.org.tr) has published a booklet entitled *Barrier-Free Istanbul for All* and appears to be making some effort to provide access information for visitors.

For general travel advice you can try contacting the following organisations:

RADAR The principal UK forum and pressure group for people with disabilities. ⓣ 020 7250 3222 (UK) ⓦ www.radar.org.uk

Society for Accessible Travel & Hospitality (SATH) Advises US-based travellers with disabilities. ⓣ 212 447 7284 (US) ⓦ www.sath.org

TOURIST INFORMATION

Tourist Information Offices:

Atatürk International Airport ⓐ International arrivals hall ⓣ (0212) 465 3547/3151 ⓑ 24 hrs

Elmadağı ⓐ Off Cumhuriyet Caddesi, in front of the Hilton Hotel ⓣ (0212) 233 0592 ⓑ 24 hrs

Karaköy ⓐ International Maritime Passenger Terminal ⓣ (0212) 249 5776 ⓑ 09.00–17.00 Mon–Sat

Sultanahmet ⓐ Divan Yolu Caddesi, northeast end of the Hippodrome ⓣ (0212) 518 8754 ⓑ 09.00–17.00 Mon–Sat

The following official tourist board website provides helpful information and useful links: ⓦ www.gototurkey.co.uk

BACKGROUND READING

Belshazzar's Daughter by Barbara Nadel. The first of a number of detective stories set in Istanbul by the British crime writer. Others include *A Chemical Prison*, *Arabesk*, *Deep Waters*, *Harem* and *Petrified*.

Constantinople by Edmondo De Amicis. 'A travel book for grown-ups' according to Orhan Pamuk and the 'best book written about Istanbul'.

Istanbul by Orhan Pamuk. Memoir and cultural history by Turkey's most famous writer, winner of the 2006 Nobel Prize for Literature.

Emergencies

The following are emergency phone numbers:

Ambulance (for state hospitals) ☎ 112

Fire ☎ 110

Police ☎ 155

Plans are under way to make all emergency numbers accessible by dialling ☎ 112. Check with the tourist office on arrival.

MEDICAL SERVICES

For emergency medical attention, use one of the city's excellent private hospitals. The German Hospital also has an eye and dental clinic.

American Hospital ⊜ Güzelbahçe Sokak 20, Nişantaşı ☎ (0212) 444 3777/311 2000 (24 hrs)

German Hospital ⊜ Sıraselviler Caddesi 119, Taksim ☎ (0212) 293 2150

POLICE

Police on motorbikes, the so-called 'dolphin police', are a rapid-response force, while the ones with white caps are traffic police. Tourist police, bearing the emblem 'Polis – Turizm', are specially trained to communicate with visitors in various languages and help with everyday problems. The main **Tourist Police Station** (⊜ Yerebatan Caddesi 6 ☎ (0212) 527 4504) is in Sultanahmet, opposite the Basilica Cistern, but other branches are currently opening around the city. Any police officer will help in an emergency.

For general lost property contact the Tourist Police Station or, for property left on public transport, visit or contact the **Karaköy Gar building** (⊜ Rıhtım Caddesi, Karaköy ☎ (0212) 245 0720).

EMERGENCY PHRASES

Help!	Fire!	Stop!
İmdat/Yardım!	Yangın!	Dur!
Imdat/Yardaem!	*Yanghen!*	*Door!*

Call an ambulance/a doctor/the police/the fire brigade!
Ambulans/doktor/polis/ıtfaiyeyi çağırın!
Ambulance/doctor/polees/itfaa-ye chaaren!

EMBASSIES & CONSULATES

Australia 🏠 Ritz Carlton residences, Asker Ocağı Caddesi 15, Elmadağ, Şişli ☎ (0212) 243 1333 🌐 www.turkey.embassy.gov.au

Canada 🏠 İstiklal Caddesi 189/5, Beyoğlu ☎ (0212) 251 9838 🌐 www.turkey.gc.ca

France 🏠 İstiklal Caddesi 8, Taksim ☎ (0212) 334 8730 🌐 www.consulfrance-istanbul.org

Germany 🏠 İsmet İnönü Caddesi 10, Gümüşsuyu ☎ (0212) 334 6100 🌐 www.istanbul.diplo.de

New Zealand 🏠 İnönü Caddesi 48, Taksim ☎ (0212) 244 0272 🌐 www.nzembassy.com

Republic of Ireland 🏠 Uğur Mumcu Caddesi 88, MNG Binası, B Blok Kat 3, Gaziosmanpasa, Ankara ☎ (0312) 446 6172 🌐 www.embassyofireland.org.tr

UK 🏠 Meşrutiyet Caddesi 34, Tepebaşı ☎ (0212) 334 6400 🌐 http://ukinturkey.fco.gov.uk

US 🏠 Kaplıcalar Mevkii 2, İstinye ☎ (0212) 335 9000 🌐 http://turkey.usembassy.gov

ACKNOWLEDGEMENTS

Thomas Cook Publishing wishes to thank SEAN SHEEHAN, to whom the copyright belongs, for the photographs in this book, except for the following images:

123RF.com (Cornel Achirei PixAchi.com, pages 40–41; maxfx, page 133; Cenap Refik Ongan, page 119); Alamy (Rebecca Erol, page 109; Richard Wareham Fotografie, page 123); Dreamstime.com (Baloncici, page 141; Evren Kalinbacak, page 87; Halilo, page 112; Jdanne, page 25; Josephboz, page 143; Katatonia82, page 32; Michal Kram, page 79; Mikhail Nekrasov, page 42; Polartern, page 29; Ukrphoto, page 19; Vesparulez, page 45); iStockphoto.com (Peeter Viisimaa, page 7; Yusuf Anil Akduygu, pages 8–9); Sarnıç Hotel, page 38; SXC.hu (Suat Gursozlu, pages 137 & 149; Ugur Vidinligil, page 127); Turkish Culture & Tourism Office, pages 5, 17, 31, 57, 65, 95, 107, 115, 120 & 131.

For CAMBRIDGE PUBLISHING MANAGEMENT LIMITED:
Project Editor: Kate Taylor
Layout: Sarah Channing-Wright
Proofreaders: Sara Chare & Karolin Thomas

Send your thoughts to
books@thomascook.com

- Found a great bar, club, shop or must-see sight that we don't feature?
- Like to tip us off about any information that needs a little updating?
- Want to tell us what you love about this handy little guidebook and more importantly how we can make it even handier?

Then here's your chance to tell all! Send us ideas, discoveries and recommendations today and then look out for your valuable input in the next edition of this title.

Email the above address (stating the title) or write to:
pocket guides Series Editor, Thomas Cook Publishing, PO Box 227, Coningsby Road, Peterborough PE3 8SB, UK.

WHAT'S IN YOUR GUIDEBOOK?

Independent authors Impartial up-to-date information from our travel experts who meticulously source local knowledge.

Experience Thomas Cook's 165 years in the travel industry and guidebook publishing enriches every word with expertise you can trust.

Travel know-how Thomas Cook has thousands of staff working around the globe, all living and breathing travel.

Editors Travel-publishing professionals, pulling everything together to craft a perfect blend of words, pictures, maps and design.

You, the traveller We deliver a practical, no-nonsense approach to information, geared to how you really use it.

Useful phrases

English	Turkish	Approx pronunciation

BASICS

English	Turkish	Approx pronunciation
Yes	Evet	Evet
No	Hayır	Hayer
Please	Lütfen	Lewtfen
Thank you	Teşekkür ederim	Teshekkuer ederim
Hello	Merhaba	Merhaba
Goodbye	Hoşçakal	Hoshcha kal
Excuse me	Affedersiniz	Afeadehrseeneez
Sorry	Pardon	Pahr-dohn
That's okay	Tamam	Taa-mam
I don't speak Turkish	Türkçe bilmiyorum	Turkche beelmiiorum
Do you speak English?	İngilizce biliyor musunuz?	Inghilizh'dje biliyour musunuz?
Good morning	Günaydın	Guenayden
Good afternoon	Merhaba	Merhaba
Good evening	İyi akşamlar	Iyi akshamlar
Goodnight	İyi geceler	Iyi gedjeler
My name is ...	Adım ...	Adaem ...

NUMBERS

English	Turkish	Approx pronunciation
One	Bir	Beer
Two	İki	Eki
Three	Üç	Uech
Four	Dört	Doert
Five	Beş	Besh
Six	Altı	Alte
Seven	Yedi	Yedi
Eight	Sekiz	Sekiz
Nine	Dokuz	Dokuz
Ten	On	On
Twenty	Yirmi	Yirmi
Fifty	Elli	Elli
One hundred	Yüz	Yuez

SIGNS & NOTICES

English	Turkish	Approx pronunciation
Airport	Havaalanı	Hava a'lane
Railway station	İstasyon	Istasyon
Platform	Peron	Peron
Smoking/No smoking	Sigara içilir/içilmez	Sigara echilir/echilmez
Toilets	Tuvaletler	Tuvaletler
Ladies/Gentlemen	Bayanlar/Erkekler	Baianlar/Erkekler
Metro/Bus	Metro/Otobüs	Metro/Otobews